TOOLS *for* HEALING

TOOLS for HEALING

Working toward Harmony and Balance

KATHY MENGLE

DEVORSS & COMPANY
P.O. BOX 550, MARINA DEL REY, CA 90294-0550

ACKNOWLEDGMENTS

I would like to thank Deborah Stauffer for her painstaking efforts in preparing the illustrations.

I first learned of Reflexology from Gloria Polson. In the years since, as my knowledge has grown, she has often volunteered to undergo various treatments. Her careful and thoughtful analyses helped me refine each mode of therapy and helped to determine what would be useful in an introductory volume.

I am also indebted to Hedda Lark, my editor at DeVorss, who shaped a good text into something even better.

CONTENTS

1

HOW HEALING WORKS

Health is the presence of balanced energies within the physical body and within the etheric body, which both interpenetrates and surrounds the physical. Such balance depends upon the cooperation and integration of all aspects of the self—physical, emotional, mental, and spiritual. Each aspect, indeed, has its own aura, and gifted clairvoyants can read the entire aura and detect imbalances long before they manifest as clinically recognizable diseases.

Most of us are, in fact, constantly working on our own health. Some of the time we are aware of it, but much of the time we are not.

Everything we do affects our energies, and anything which helps us balance our energies and keep them in or near a state of equilibrium fosters health. Anything which unbalances the energies saps the body in the present and prevents it from building up energy reserves which may be called upon in the future.

So, if you know that certain habits (or even attitudes) unbalance your energies, and you still choose to keep those habits, no outside healing agent is going to be able to make you well. A workaholic who will not rest or exercise or become emotionally involved with others cannot be made healthy by voluminous amounts of vitamins. By our first definition, only a *balanced* lifestyle can offer the opportunity for health. And only you can choose health.

By the same token, you cannot make others choose health, and that is one of the hardest lessons for any of us to learn. Neither can you make others well. But if they have chosen to get well, then you can help them to achieve that goal faster. All healing is truly self-healing, but an extra input of energy can speed up the healing process. The person who really wants to be whole can open himself or herself up to many sources of healing energies, including all of those discussed in this book.

A person who is very ill, however, may exhaust all of his or her resources just to maintain basic functioning and to keep from getting any worse. Such people have no energy reserves and usually welcome outside help. If you know how, you can give others energy and help them grow strong enough so that eventually they will make their own reserves and move toward full health again.

Physical illness is not the only danger. It is simply the most socially acceptable. Consequently, frustrations on other levels of being are often disguised and ignored until they eventually manifest as physical illness. Stomach ulcers produced by anger have become commonplace. So in working for healing, it is less important to remove a symptom than it is to work toward balance, and this has increasingly become my approach.

By giving another person extra energy, we allow his entire system to move toward self-healing. Results may be slow; sometimes they are immediate. Sometimes symptoms are peeled away, one at a time, until the real source of discomfort is uncovered. It may be standing too long in the wrong kind of shoes, or it may go much deeper, to a long-standing fear or resentment or to feelings of inadequacy. At every step of the way, healing can occur only if the person involved truly wants it and is ready for it.

There are two huge stumbling blocks which often get in the way of our health and development. The biggest danger, perhaps, is comfort, because when we feel comfortable and secure, we try to perpetuate that security, and we become fearful of anyone or anything which seems to threaten our comfort. So the second stumbling block is fear, because it drives us backward rather than forward.

The Universe is not resting on its laurels. The Universe is changing and moving, and it requires movement and change from us. The ultimate security, then, comes from realizing and developing fully all of the different aspects of ourselves so that we can welcome change and deal with it comfortably and successfully.

You will find that, whether you are working on yourself or on others, change and adaptability are necessary. Both are essential ingredients of growth. By accepting the need to stretch yourself, you also become more open toward and more accepting of others, and that, in itself, constitutes a great step forward in self-healing.

The first part of this book emphasizes practical methods that you can begin to use, today, to bring your body and life back into harmony with the Universe.

The second part of the book presents four systems of healing which can be applied either to oneself or to others. The effectiveness of these systems is dependent upon many things: the skill of the practitioner; the willingness of the person to be healed; the person's general level of energy; and the acceptance, by the individual involved, of responsibility for personal growth and health.

These healing methods have worked for others, and they will work for you. As your knowledge and understanding of them grows, so will your ability to help others. Attitude is everything. The more you experience success, the more you will believe; and the more you believe, the more successful you will be. In this case, the cycle is not vicious. Indeed, you may find that it is miraculous.

These and other methods work in several different ways: 1) directly on the underlying structures [massage, polarity]; 2) through body reflexes [acupressure, massage, Shiatsu, Am-ma, Do-In, reflexology, polarity]; 3) via acupuncture meridian flow [acupressure, polarity]; 4) by encouraging the production and release of the body's natural pain killers (endorphins are five to ten times stronger than morphine, and can produce calmness, euphoria, and joy) [Shiatsu, polarity, reflexology, acupressure]; 5) by assisting the body in its normal flow of fluids and energies [all]; and 6) by removing blockages from the energy flow around the body [all].

The methods presented are easy to learn and can safely be used by any conscientious person.

Here are two further rules of thumb: 1) When in doubt, don't; and 2) It is always safe to use polarity, staying one-half inch away from the body.

WARNING: THE METHODS DESCRIBED HEREIN ARE NO SUBSTITUTE FOR MEDICAL CARE. ALWAYS SEEK APPROPRIATE MEDICAL DIAGNOSIS AND TREATMENT.

2

EXERCISE:

MOVING YOUR BODY

There are many rewards in fitness. Exercise is good for you, if you follow a careful and informed regimen. Exercise improves the circulation, which stimulates the flow of blood and lymph, bringing both nutrients and housecleaners to each part of the body more easily than they can travel under sedentary conditions. This helps the body function more efficiently, and the reward is that you end up with extra energy for other pursuits. Notice the people around you: those who do not move are always tired, while those who move a great deal have almost limitless reserves. One reason for this is that exercise also helps to move out the chemicals produced during the stresses of your daily life; when you do not exercise, they are stored in the body as wastes, and clog your system.

WALKING AS EXERCISE

If you are out of shape or have never followed an exercise program, begin by walking. Walking is basic, but it is also excellent for everyone: it is considered one of the eight best all-around exercises, and one of the four best for weight control. Start slowly, with fifteen minutes a day, and work up to gradually faster paces, and then longer times. Try to walk in the open air, and be alert to your surroundings. If you pay attention, you'll be surprised, at the end of the first week, at how much you've learned about yourself and the neighborhood.

It is prudent to check with your physician before beginning a more rigorous program. Laurence E. Morehouse, in *Total Fitness in 30 Minutes A Week*, has outlined a program which can easily be tailored to suit your personal preferences.

If you want to use walking as your aerobic exercise, you need a minimum of fifteen to twenty minutes of rapid walking three times a week. This should be preceded by five to ten minutes of stretching exercises to warm up the body, and your walk should be followed by another five to ten minutes for cooling down at a more relaxed pace. [Aerobic exercise produces a heart rate that is 70-to-85% of your maximum. Subtract your age from 220, and check your pulse periodically to see if you're on target. Remember to start slow and work your way up to your ideal level of fitness. Example: 220 – 50 years old = 170; 170 x .7 = 119.0; 170 x .85 = 144.50. So you want your pulse rate to eventually reach 119 to 144 beats per minute. The easiest way to figure your pulse is to count it—using a watch—for six seconds, and then multiply that number by ten.]

Enjoy whatever exercises you have chosen, and get in touch with your physical body. Feel the muscles and joints responding. Pay attention to the flow of air into and out of your lungs. Feel your blood moving faster as your heart steps up its pace. Let yourself open up to the Universe and feel at one with it. Try to keep that feeling of connectedness and oneness flowing throughout the rest of your day.

If your schedule permits, keep on with your walking program even after starting more intensive exercise. There is something subtle in walking that belies its simplicity.

In most of our daily activities, we move without even thinking about it. Usually, we bend, stretch, or lift automatically. We move from habit. Healing therapies, however, often demand unusual motions or more strenuous movements than those used in ordinary life.

In doing massage, we often need to move our bodies and our body weight from one point to another in order to continue a long stroke covering several portions of the body. We attain the fluidity to move the body gracefully through constant repetition, until all of the muscles and nerves are so precisely coordinated that the movement seems effortless.

In polarity, we do not need as much movement, but we are often stretching between distant points on the body and we must learn how to do this effortlessly, too, so that the body can remain relaxed and maintain the position indefinitely. Tension in the body, or tiredness as the session progresses, inhibits the flow of energy.

STRETCHING EXERCISES

There are numerous exercises which can help you increase your flexibility and acquire the agility to move so that you get maximum effectiveness from minimal movement. Stretching exercises used by martial artists or by dancers are particularly good. The exercises which follow are basic, and fairly easy to do.

It's a good idea to get into the habit of stretching before giving any treatments. If you can, get your partner to stretch along with you for a few minutes. We often forget how lovely it feels to move the body slowly and gently. Stretching also helps you and your partner loosen up the muscles of the back and ribcage so that you can both breathe deeply during the session.

1) WARM-UP
Raise your arms overhead. Then lower your hands to the floor, bending the knees slightly. Now lower your buttocks into a squat. Next stretch your hips upward. Then gently unwind your back, vertebra by vertebra, till you have returned to the starting position. Repeat two times. Do this anytime during the day when you notice tension building up in your body.

2) SQUATS

There are many squatting positions, and they are good for stretching, but may take some getting used to. Start slowly (fifteen seconds) and work your way up to longer durations (three minutes or so). In parts of the world where chairs are scarce, the people spend a great deal of time squatting.

3) OPPOSITE TOE TOUCH

Stand with your feet thirty-six inches apart. Raise your arms to the side at shoulder level. Alternating your arms, bend over and try to touch the opposite toes. Bending slightly at the knees is recommended.

4) STATIONARY STRETCH

Start with your feet parallel and thirty-six inches or more apart —whatever distance is comfortable. Now point your right foot outward, away from you, and bend your right knee. Bend as far as you can comfortably, while keeping the left leg straight, and hold to a count of ten. Straighten your right leg and turn your right foot back to its original position. Now point your left foot out, and do the same exercise to the left. Repeat this entire sequence twice more. As you become more proficient, widen the distance between your feet, and then lengthen the duration of the hold.

5) PLANTED FEET

Begin with your feet parallel and twenty-four to thirty-six inches apart. Bend your knees slightly. Slowly move as far to the right as you can, without moving your feet. Then move to the left. Repeat to each side four more times.

6) MOVING STRETCH

Have your feet parallel and thirty to thirty-six inches apart. Move your right foot 90° outward and bend your right knee.

Move the left foot about 45° inward, keeping the left leg straight. Stretch as far as you can to the right, balancing your weight between your left hip and your right thigh. Then slowly shift your weight and straighten the right leg as you bend the left knee. You should now be able to feel your weight in the left foot and the right heel. Pivot around until your left foot is outward 90° and your right foot is inward 45°. Stretch as far as you can to the left. Repeat at least twice to each side.

7) PELVIC STRETCH

Have your feet eighteen to twenty-four inches apart and then slowly squat. Use your arms, bent at the elbow, to force your thighs further apart. Do this gently! The further you can stretch, the better. The longer you can stay in this position, the better. When you get really adventuresome, rock your weight from one side to the other, then forward and back, and finally in a circle, first in one direction and then in the other. This is wonderful for loosening muscles in the pelvic area. It is also good for the lower back and the legs.

All of these will help you glide more easily between positions or aid you in maintaining difficult postures. As you become more aware of postures and movements, you will find yourself using these exercise motions in your work and personal life.

3

MEDITATION
AND VISUALIZATION

Meditation can result in complete relaxation, mental tranquility, increased energy, and stress reduction. During correct meditation, the brain wave pattern reflects complete freedom from stress. Consequently, correct meditation will result in well-being at all levels.

Meditation is really quite simple, if you follow a few rules. Wait at least two hours after eating. Choose a time of day when you are not fatigued. Wear comfortable clothing so that you can relax completely. Choose a quiet place where you will not be disturbed. Unplug the telephone. Sit upright in a chair, with your head erect. Twenty minutes is a maximum time in the beginning. (I began with just five minutes a day, years ago, and gradually increased the time as I became more used to the process of quieting myself and learning to concentrate.) If you have a busy schedule, meditate first thing in the morning. Try to practice regularly, once a day, for a month. Then reflect upon how you feel now versus how you felt a month ago.

There are many ways to meditate, but they all fall into two basic categories: meditation with seed, and meditation without seed. In meditation with seed, you close your eyes and focus your mind on something—on a virtue, an idea, a thought, the rhythm of your breathing, or the content of your fleeting thoughts. In meditation without seed, you close your eyes and rest for twenty minutes. Both methods are suitable for stress reduction and increased health. Many schools of thought, however, believe it is important to train the mind to concentrate, and seeds help do this. Seeds are a means of inducing mental clarity. So the distinction here is growth. Meditation without seed will improve your health. Meditation with seed will aid you in gradually discovering hitherto unknown aspects of yourself.

Do not expect revelations from your meditative time. Simply relax. You may want to begin with seedless meditation until you develop the habit; and practicing at the same time every day will make it easier to remember. You might even begin to look forward to these private, peaceful moments. Many people find that as their stress level diminishes, their creativity begins to soar.

Rest for a few moments afterwards, before resuming your regular activities. Enjoy the calmness which you have achieved.

There is one further important consideration here. Go inward when you meditate. Leave your worries, frustrations, problems, and concerns from the outer world behind. They will still be there when you return, but the refreshed, post-meditation you can look at them with clearer vision and perhaps even discover some new and better ways of dealing with the rest of your life. You will not derive maximum benefit from the meditative periods unless you leave your stresses behind; until you can, you will simply be worrying hard with your eyes closed!

MEDITATIVE SEEDS

1. I am One with the Universe.

2. Love, Joy, Peace, and so on. All virtues and positive emotions, as well as uplifting ideas.

3. In quietness, I find my Self.

4. I am in harmony with Life.

VISUALIZATION

Visualization is mental-picturing, the "seeing" of things in "the mind's eye." It can be used for many different purposes—either by itself, or in conjunction with other methods. Visualization is often combined with planning, and it can be used, as well, with affirmations, meditations, sports performances, and many healing practices. If "thinking makes it so," visualization is the motion picture of the thought, the image of your dream being materialized.

Some people find visualization easy, while others find it next to impossible. Everyone can get better at it with practice, and the correct use of visualization can bring many benefits.

More and more athletes are using visualization for "mental practice," as distinct from physical workouts. In mental practice, the athlete sees himself or herself giving a perfect performance. Astonishingly, this trains the body to respond appropriately, and physical performance improves. Thus, during off-seasons or whenever events or injuries or travel prevent physical training sessions, training can continue mentally. The ideal, of course, is to be able to do both mental and physical practice. This enables the athlete to both think sharply and to feel sharp physically and thereby guarantees the best possible performance.

The difference between ordinary imaginings and visualization is intent. We imagine very many things kaleidoscopically and briefly: they are there, we toy with them, we get distracted by something new, we toy with that, and so on. We imaginatively try things on for size and then proceed with life. In visualization, however, we focus on one idea or event, and perfect the scene as we want it to happen, and then rehearse it over and over until—correct!—it has become a new habit which we can perform easily.

You can devise your own program(s) suited to your needs, and you can alter the program(s) whenever necessary. You can see yourself being strong and decisive, or choosing more healthy options for yourself, or changing to better habits, or successfully completing your work assignments on schedule. You can even rehearse behaviors and events for establishing better interpersonal relationships. And yes, you can use visualization to converse with and connect various parts of yourself.

I use visualization all the time. When I write fiction or drama, I see the scene before me. In meditation, I draw pictures or see the working out of some idea or insight. I picture relationships moving toward a more perfect ideal. (This is easy, because we are all always moving and changing, and therefore our relationships are, too.) I visualize extensively the person I want to become, and the behaviors I must develop in order to fulfill that ideal. When doing massage, I picture the nerves and muscles relaxing as I work on them. I always visualize energy when I am using polarity or doing any channeling. Visualizing helps me focus my attention, for both short- and long-term results.

Visualization is *Willing*. However, the correct preparation is necessary. You must establish the right foundation for what you want to accomplish. Then, the more prepared you are, and the more realistic the images become, and the more you believe, the faster your visualization will become reality. (Realistic images are ones picturing yourself in the actual place, giving your performance, with every possible detail included—your attire, the judges, the audience, etc.) Obviously, in order to give a flawless performance, you must deserve one. But if you have sufficiently developed all the necessary basic skills, and then have diligently practiced until you have mastered every part of your planned presentation, then visualization can pay off by giving added confidence, which may lift you into a level of performance where everything flows perfectly.

Anyone who needs to develop or maintain a particular skill can use visualization to advantage; this would include such people as dancers, musicians, dentists, surgeons, athletes, and race car drivers.

VISUALIZATION EXERCISES

It is easier to remain alert, but relaxed, in an upright position; it takes much more effort to visualize while lying down—most people have a tendency to fall asleep in a prone position. So sit on a straight-backed chair, with your feet flat on the floor and your hands resting comfortably about mid-thigh. Close your eyes, and take at least three deep breaths, and let your body relax as completely as possible. You are now ready to try one of the following exercises. [You can, if you wish, tape them ahead of time for use during your visualization period. However, these are fairly simple to imagine, and you may be able to relax more fully without the distraction of a tape recorder.]

A. Return in your mind to your favorite beach. Imagine yourself traveling there, and once you arrive, see yourself lying on the beach, with no one else around. The Sun is shining overhead, and you feel its penetrating rays gently warming you. Take a moment to enjoy this scene. Then, as you lie on the sand, slowly concentrate on your entire body, beginning with your feet. See each foot relax, as you begin to breathe more deeply. Then each ankle relaxes, then each calf, each shin, each knee, each thigh, each buttock, the lower back, the mid-back, the upper back, the lower abdomen, the upper abdomen, the chest, the hands, the arms, the shoulders, the neck, the face, and the scalp. Now see your whole body completely relaxed and soaking up the healing energies radiating down from the Sun. Enjoy that feeling for as long as you like. When you are ready, slowly stretch and get up and leave the beach and travel back to present time. If you can, allow yourself to leisurely return to your normal activities.

B. Return in your mind to a favorite place in the mountains. You are completely safe here, and again, solitude is yours for as long as you desire it. You stretch out in a grassy meadow, with your hands behind your head, looking up at the few clouds overhead which are thinly obscuring the summer Sun's rays. Inhale the crisp mountain air, and let it linger in your lungs as you breathe slowly and deeply, inhaling and exhaling evenly. You gradually feel at one with the rhythms of the Universe, and your whole body feels weightless, as though perfectly buoyed up by the Earth beneath you. You know that if you wish, you can become one with the clouds or the Sun or any of the large pine trees in the surrounding forest. When you are ready to return to present time, you slowly see yourself coming out of the forest, down the mountains, and back to your home. Allow yourself to leisurely return to normal duties.

C. Along the seashore, or up in the mountains, return in memory to a waterfall you once enjoyed in person. See yourself traveling there, and finally arriving. Sit on a bench or on the ground where you will have a safe but clear view of the waterfall.

Concentrate first on the water itself, flowing downward freely, coming forward, but not rushing itself—flowing along with the rest of Nature. You, too, can be like the water, ever-moving but also ever-harmonious with your surroundings.

Notice next the light being reflected by the water. The water itself is crystal clear, but as it moves, it can become white or brown or cream or green. What other colors appear? Is there a rainbow anywhere in the waterfall? Are you, like the water, able to reflect a multitude of colors to those around you? Are you working to make yourself crystal clear, or are there obstructions within you that have been muddying your clarity? Even if you are mostly clear, is there anything that you could do that would enable you to create an even more radiant rainbow in your environment? Only you know, and only you can choose your radiance, moment by moment.

Next, look closely at the edges of the pool into which the water drops. Along the edges, small pools of water sometimes become isolated. In time, their vitality is absorbed by plants and animals as the life chain continues. Each of us chooses whether to live in the mainstream of the waterfall, or along the edges of it. We can live, and grow, and make a contribution to the greater life, in either place. Other forms of life are carried by "Chance," and strive to live wherever they find themselves. Only humans can choose their lives and their surroundings and their work with any real degree of freedom. Reflect a few moments on your own life, on the contributions you are making or could be making.

When you have been totally refreshed by the negative ions of the free-running water, slowly travel back from the waterfall to your home. Return leisurely to your ordinary pursuits.

Each of the foregoing exercises can put you in touch with nearly-forgotten aspects of yourself. You may remember experiences which you had totally put aside for years. You might recall childhood joys with a freshness long-gone. Other memories may begin knocking on the door of your conscious mind in days or weeks ahead. Savor them, and learn from them.

Each exercise above is designed to help you create a level of relaxation or healing or understanding which you can tap into at will during "ordinary" times. By remembering yourself on the sand, you can call forth healing energies from the Sun to work in your body anytime, anyplace. By recalling the mountain meadow, you can be at one with the Universe no matter what your external circumstances are. By thinking again about the water, you can decide whether or not you belong in the mainstream during this phase of your growth.

Once you have experienced these basic exercises using visualization, you can begin creating your own, and you can tailor them to your personal needs.

There are certain other "half-planned" exercises which you may also choose to try. Allow yourself plenty of time.

Hall of Silence. In the middle of a large city, you discover yourself suddenly on the steps of a huge stone building. You push open a small wooden door and step inside. The door closes quietly behind you. The lighting is soft, and you sit on a bench there in the outer chamber. This is an immense building, and in the central area, you see a fair number of people busily working. You breathe deeply and feel very peaceful here. The air is clean and crisp and clear. Only gradually do you realize that everything here is silent. All the city noises have remained outside; and everyone here works intently, but quietly.

Wise Old Person. You take a walk in the country, and eventually stop to rest. You sit on a large tree stump and notice all the surroundings—clouds, trees, grass, insects, sunshine, breezes. Just as you're about to leave, you hear someone coming along the path. This person comes into view, and you immediately recognize him or her as a very wise person. You are elated about this chance meeting, and invite the wise person to sit down by you. You may ask this person any questions you have—even thorny philosophical ones.

Guidance. You walk along a beach and approach a park where there are trees and bushes. You sit down to rest and begin pon-

dering some question in your life. Suddenly you hear a quiet rus-
tling in the leaves behind you, and you turn slowly to see what
is approaching. It may be a person; it may be an animal. Invite it
to stay, and make friends with it. It has come to bring you
guidance or insight so that you can effectively solve the problem
before you.

Healing.   You enter a temple, and then, down a hallway, you
find a Healing Room. You enter this room, and discover many
crystals inside it, suspended from the ceiling. You can feel the
power of the crystals permeating the room. You may receive sudden insight into the origin of the condition for which you seek
healing. You are welcome to remain here until you feel certain
that healing has been achieved on the inner levels of your being.
Such healing will manifest physically in a matter of days or
months. There is a table in the middle of the room, and you are
welcome to lie on this table in order to absorb the healing rays of
the crystals. Be thankful for any insights as well as the healing
energies.

Treasure Chest.   You are walking along a deserted seashore,
and suddenly come upon a cove. It becomes obvious to you that
several centuries ago, a shipwreck occurred near here. The water
in the cove is a beautiful pale blue. You enjoy this scene for a few
moments, and then walk on. As you start to ascend the path on
the other side of the cove, your eye is suddenly caught by the
reflection of sunlight on something metallic, just off the path to
your right, toward the open sea. You kneel down and discover
that hidden in the sand is a treasure chest. The metal on the corner
of it has been uncovered. Your heart races as you begin scooping
away sand so that you can open the chest. Will it be empty? Will it
contain anything of value? You are both optimistic and skeptical,
and so, to quiet your heart, you try to become detached. You
silently ask that, since the chest was brought into your life, that it
might contain something which can be of value to your life (this

could include just about anything—even an idea, or generalized wisdom). You take a deep breath, and slowly open the lid. If you wish, you may call upon someone from the *Wise Old Person* or *Guidance* exercises to help you understand the full and deeper meanings of all the contents of your treasure chest.

It is always a good idea to write down the results of any visualizations. You may want to draw what you saw. Doing this helps sharpen your perceptions, and provides a good record which you may consult later, either to check for details, or just to re-read and savor.

4

CRYSTALS

Crystals are available in many shapes, sizes, and colors. They are used in various ways for different purposes. The ordinary clear rock quartz crystal found in many rock and hobby shops and in some jewelry stores is pointed on one end and is therefore called a single terminate.

Double terminates—those having both ends pointed—are also available, but are more rare, and so are more expensive.

Clusters are combined crystals which stand together. They may or may not emerge from a single base. Occasionally you will find just two crystals joined, but it is much more common to find three or more crystals in a cluster.

Many people believe that the right crystal appears when you are ready for one. The clear crystal is preferable for beginners, because it contains all the colors of the spectrum and therefore can help alleviate all conditions.

Put time and effort into choosing your crystal. Look the stones over carefully, and pick up, one at a time, those which strike your eye. Use your intuition while holding each crystal. Keep trying the ones you like until you determine which one feels best to you. You will choose the one that is most compatible with your vibrations.

Cleansing the crystal is easy. Scrub it with an old brush in warm water. Then soak it in warm salt water for ten minutes; this will disperse any negativity it may have acquired. Dry it off, expose it to the Sun for one hour, and it is ready to use.

Use the crystal for short periods initially. It does amplify or multiply energy, and it may take you several weeks to acclimate yourself to the presence of the crystal. You can hold your crystal, or wear it on your person. Consider it your friend. Learn how to use it wisely, and it will become an extension of yourself.

You can receive or send energies. If you want to receive energy, simply hold the crystal in the palm of your left hand with the point facing toward your body. Close your fingers and gently hold the crystal in a loose fist.

To send energy into a particular part of your body, or even to another person, for healing, hold the crystal in your right hand with the point facing away from you. Held in this way, the crystal can be used to direct energy into any point on the body and can be used in polarity holds or in acupressure treatments [hold the crystal on the point, but do not press!].

Be careful when using crystals. They are not toys. It is always better to understimulate than to overstimulate yourself or someone else. Overstimulation can result in agitation, headache, nausea, or acute discomfort.

Try holding the crystal in your left hand, with the point toward you, during meditation, to increase your attunement to your inner self. You can also use the crystal to amplify your intention and effort when doing visualization or affirmations.

Remember that the crystal is a sort of magnifying glass. It, in itself, is an impartial conveyor of energy. Make certain that your thoughts when using the crystal are harmless and constructive, because what you send out will be returned to you *multiplied* (by a factor of three or more).

It is fine for others to hold or touch your crystal. If you sense any negativity after others have handled it, bathe it again in the salt water solution.

As you change, so do your energy levels, and you may from time to time want to acquire additional crystals which will match your new energies. Continue to choose them in the same way.

Some people like to keep all the crystals which have held meaning for them, while others prefer to sell, trade, or give away crystals which they have outgrown.

Meditation With Crystals

Sit in a comfortable position, with your back straight. Hold your crystal in your left hand, with the point facing toward you. Fold your fingers over gently to create a loose fist.

Close your eyes and take three deep breaths, inhaling slowly through the nose and exhaling through either your nose or mouth. Feel your body relaxing.

Say the following dis-identification mantram:

"I have a body, but I am not my body;
I have emotions, but I am not my emotions;
I have thoughts, but I am not my thoughts;
I am the eternal soul, working through these external vehicles."

Picture your crystal inverted and expanding until it is twelve feet high and six feet wide. Picture a door in the crystal. Beyond the door, you will find an appropriate building for meditation. Walk up to the door and open it and step through to the other side. Be aware. Note everything you see, hear, think, feel.

Walk toward the edifice in front of you and enter it. Notice your surroundings. What are the dimensions of this building? What materials is it made of? Are you alone? If not, who else is there, and what is his function? Is there music? Enter the central hall, and sit or kneel for several moments to acquaint yourself with this place and to recollect why you have come here. Do you seek guidance, information, healing, self-understanding?

Then walk to the far end of the central hall, to the double doors at the far side. If you wish, you may summon a guide to go with you. Beyond the double doors is a long hallway containing the entrances to many rooms. Some of those rooms have their functions clearly marked on the doors. You might choose to visit the Healing Chamber for yourself or on behalf of someone else, or you might step into the Library. In the Computer Room you can search out any knowledge for past, present, or future. In the Vacation Room, you can travel wherever you choose. You also have the option of visiting the Practice Room, where you can rehearse whatever skills you have which you wish to develop perfectly.

There are many other possibilities behind other doors. There are Meditation Rooms and even study rooms where classes on various subjects are being taught. Stroll slowly down this hall, and gradually let yourself choose the one door which beckons you the most. Remember that you can return on subsequent days to investigate other rooms.

Open the door you have chosen, and step inside. What do you see? Sit down on a bench, and let yourself become familiar with your surroundings. You may continue on by yourself; or, if you wish, you may summon a guide or helper to assist you in your quest. Remember, however, that these guides are only here to help you understand your options; they are not permitted to influence you or make your decisions for you.

Take as long as you wish to ascertain the answers you seek. When you are ready to leave, express your thankfulness for what you have learned, and then go slowly back to the hallway and through the central chamber and outside the building. Come back through the doorway in your crystal and down to the chair where you began. See your crystal inverting itself again and becoming smaller until it fits into your hand once more.

Take three deep breaths. You may want to record your experiences in detail before resuming your ordinary activities. You may also find additional insights coming to you for the next forty-eight hours.

This meditation can be done as often as you wish.

5

THE POWER
OF SPEECH AND WORDS

Speech is one of the most overlooked influences in our lives. Yet it is profoundly important, because when we speak, we use words to transmit thoughts, meanings, feelings, and information from ourselves to others.

The other side of speaking is listening. Those who have studied hypnosis and the subconscious mind know that the subconscious is forever recording everything it hears.

It becomes worthwhile, then, to examine the sounds and words in our environment, because they are all being recorded. And the one major drawback to the almost-miraculous subconscious is that it has no censors, no screening-out devices. Since the subconscious cannot filter out unwanted influences, it becomes each individual's responsibility to choose what enters one's subconscious and to employ whatever censorship or corrective modes one deems necessary.

Everything that is heard by the conscious and the subconscious minds is processed and acted upon. For example, the conscious mind hears a political announcement, and, depending upon your political inclinations, the conscious either accepts or rejects the information that has been provided. If you are listening attentively and agree with the message, you might process the conscious in-

24

formation, "That's right. I intend to vote for that person."

What happens many times, though, is that we automatically accept whatever enters the subconscious without weighing it. This happens any time we fall asleep in front of the radio, TV, stereo, or other entertainment equipment. And the same thing applies to anything we overhear—on an airplane, a bus, or even in a restaurant. Indeed, it has been proven that we begin recording at the moment of conception, so that whatever the prospective mother hears is implanted in the fetus. Consequently, the subconscious has heard a great deal of information which may or may not be true, or which may no longer be true.

The solution to this information dilemma is not to somehow replay all those tapes which your subconscious has so conscientiously stored for you all these years, but rather to take a much more active interest in what you hear and process from this moment on. Ordinary listening scatters your forces and focus; attentive listening (censorship) helps you educate the subconscious and control the focus of its attention.

There are several ways to recover the power of speech and hearing. All of them require you to take an active part in choosing what will enter your recording system henceforth.

1. *Silence.* Take some time every day to be quiet, to gather your own thoughts and look them over, to reach your own conclusions. At first, you may decide that you've been unduly influenced by everyone but yourself. Relax. You're in a position to begin changing that now. You might make lists of items that are and are not important to you. Thinking things over will put you in touch with your own values.

Some spiritual traditions, both Eastern and Western, place a great deal of emphasis on silence. There are two good reasons. Silence helps interrupt the usual chatter in your own mind (or at least helps you become aware of it!) and it de-emphasizes speech as a communication tool with others. There are, after all, several alternatives to speech. Many common meanings can be conveyed between people merely through glances, smiles, or gestures combining the eyes, face, and hands. People who live together or work together often become intuitive about each other, based on these gesture-patterns. We even notice the absence of these patterns when we decide, "So-and-so has been acting strange lately. I wonder what's bothering him/her."

Another reason for silence is that it makes us more conscious of our words when we resume speaking. One thing that quickly becomes evident after a period of silence is how much more energy it takes to talk than to remain quiet. So we may become more careful of how we use all our energies, and also more careful of the number of words we use.

2. *Auditory Input.*   You now choose what you will hear. This includes all forms of entertainment and all sources of information, including mates, friends, family, neighbors, and co-workers. Evaluate these sources. Do you like what you're hearing from them? You can turn off the radio or TV. You will have to devise your own methods for dealing with the people in your life.

There are many sorts of people. Go back to your silence and evaluate the people in your surroundings. You want to eliminate—as much as you can—anything of a negative or superfluous nature. Consider what methods might work with each person. Negative people and negative subjects drain you. Discussing this with people who won't understand what you're talking about will also drain you, so avoiding people, or gradually spending less time with them, can be more helpful than trying to explain your new consciousness to an unwilling or unsympathetic listener. At work, look around for allies. Two or more of you can change the whole atmosphere of the office.

3. *Accentuating the Positive.*   There are always at least two ways to say something, if you are inventive. Most of us have ab-

sorbed negative ways of responding from parents, teachers, peers, or the culture in general. "Don't cross the street till the light turns green!" (Why not, "Wait here, and cross when the light turns green"?) "Don't touch that; it's hot!" "Don't touch that, it's poison!" "Don't play with so-and-so." "Don't let anyone touch you." "Don't accept rides with strangers." "Don't do anything without asking me first." Is it any wonder that we often find ourselves describing ourselves and our lives in the negative? Let's change, "I don't like_____" into, "I really prefer_____," or, "I really like_____."

4. *Speech.* All right, listen to yourself talk. Are you emphasizing the positive? This takes practice, because most of us have been using unexamined ways of communicating. Start building new patterns, and think before you speak. Experiment, and see if others start responding to you more positively as your speech habits change. Others may notice a change in you without being able to define it. Positivity attracts, and other people will find you more attractive. However, do not presume that your example alone will enlighten those around you in regard to speech. As you are discovering, it takes effort to change long-held patterns. It will take will-power, persistence, and time to build the new habits you want. The rewards, though, can be significant, both for yourself and those around you, because you are demonstrating in a very concrete way that you care about the quality of life that you lead and the influence you have on others.

AFFIRMATIONS

Remember the Little Engine Who Could? It used affirmations. It knew the route, knew what was required to successfully reach the top of the hill, and it maintained a positive attitude which it reinforced every time it said, "I think I can!"

Anyone can utilize this powerful method of achievement and success.

An affirmation is a carefully-chosen statement which is also a *cause* and consequently brings back a corresponding *effect*. It is very important to develop and use positive and harmless statements.

Affirmations can be written, spoken, thought, or visualized, and some people combine all these methods.

Affirmations can be prepared for any situation. And they do work! They can help you alter your life or habits or reinforce anything you already have but want to emphasize more.

Here are some guidelines to help you begin:

1. *Be Totally Positive.*   Construct your affirmations so that they are completely positive in wording and impact.

Suppose you're having a personality clash with Andy, your next-door neighbor. You could affirm, "Andy no longer bothers me," but you would still be emphasizing the element of *bother.* "I am now calm around Andy," is more positive. It gets rid of the *no* and *bother* and replaces them with *calm*, which is both peaceful and soothing. You can, if you choose, go one step further and create what I call Generic Affirmations. Such an affirmation will cover a multitude of people or events. A good one for use here would be, "I am now calm at all times," or, "I am continuously calm." Both of these take the emphasis totally away from Andy and let you concentrate on telling the Universe that you want to be surrounded by perpetual calmness.

2. *Understand Your Needs.*   Study the situation carefully until you determine what it is that you want. A momentary solution may not provide the real key to success. You will attain your goals much faster if you can focus, from the beginning, on what is truly necessary or important.

You may want a raise. Who decides whether or not you will get one? Has your work merited a raise? Whom can you influence on your behalf, if you deserve an increase in pay? On an even more important level, can you plan a better use of your present salary so that any raise you get can be invested to improve your life in some regard? Once you have thought through what you want, and know exactly why you want it, you will be able to devise the perfect affirmations.

3. *Be Precise.* If you want higher pay at work, say, "My salary has been increased to_____," or, "My salary is now _____," rather than, "I now have more money." There are, after all, many ways to have more money; you want to affirm increased earnings.

4. *Be Concise.* There is a certain temptation, in being precise, to spell everything out. Take time to distill what you want. Try to discover a Generic Affirmation, or even a Universal Affirmation: "My needs are now supplied," or, "I live in perfect harmony with the Universe." These affirmations both encompass and transcend a particular situation. And you will be able to see, soon, whether your needs are being supplied, or whether you are now living more harmoniously. If you decide that things aren't moving along quickly enough for your satisfaction, reduce the Universal or Generic to your particular situation: "I now have the_____ I need"; "My relationships are now harmonious and loving."

5. *Choose Measurable Goals.* You may say, "I will be rich by the time I retire," and you might be very right, but how are you going to gauge your progress toward that goal? Richness is relative, so be careful in choosing monetary goals. And what if you decide that you want to retire at forty, rather than sixty? How would that change your strategy for reaching both final and intermediate goals?

Select your goals carefully. Begin with ones you can believe in and measure. Then, as your proficiency increases, move on to more complex strategies.

Beginning Affirmations

I have perfect work for perfect pay.

I am now drawn to the right_____ to enrich my life. [Fill in whatever you need: people, places, jobs, circumstances, relationships, opportunities, ideas.]

I am now at peace with myself.

I can now find the perfect solution.

My needs are supplied.

Intermediate Affirmations

I now have loving relationships.

I now control my thoughts and use them constructively.

I now choose to be healthy.

I now enjoy perfect health.

Advanced Affirmations

All of the knowledge of the Universe is available to me.

I am perfect peace.

I am a channel for healing energies.

I am one with the Universe.

6. *Be Prepared for Their Fulfillment.* Every cause produces an effect. Be ready to accept and use what you have solicited from the Universe. Act as if your statement has come true. Do everything you can to help your affirmation manifest. Become more calm. Become more loving yourself. Make sure that your work is worthy of a raise. The Little Engine did not sit at home doing nothing. It did its utmost to ensure success.

7. *Share.* The more you give, the more room there is for a further inflow of abundance—whether of money, joy, peace, healing, laughter, or whatever. Everything is continuously moving. If you recognize yourself as part of the Divine Flow, ever inward and ever outward, you will know that sharing always leaves you with more than you had before you shared.

If you want to learn more about designing and using affirmations, study Marion Weinstein's excellent book, *Positive Magic.*

6

CHAKRA ENERGIES
AND HUMAN RELATIONS

Every time two people interact, an exchange of energy takes place between them. This exchange, usually unconscious, occurs between the major chakras of the individuals involved. The energy exchange is normal and natural, and to a certain extent it determines the quality of the relationship which any two people can have.

BONDING

The flow of energies between chakras helps us discover which people we would like to know better and which ones we would like to avoid entirely. When another person's energy flow from a particular chakra matches the frequency of energy from yours, a strong circuit of energy back and forth between you is established. Such circuits, while often unrecognized, help to explain some of the unusual bonding that occurs between people. Shared energy at the heart chakra, for instance, would make two individuals seem warm and loving toward each other from the moment they met.

This would not necessarily mean, however, that they were well-matched in other areas.

It is generally felt that people can establish and maintain (for a while, at least) relationships whenever there is a strong flow between them on at least three of the seven levels. Naturally, their rapport increases for every level that they share, so the deepest and longest-lasting relationships are those in which five to seven harmonies exist. At least this would seem so, in theory.

However, even an initial matching of frequencies is no guarantee of perpetual happiness. All of us are living, and moving, and changing. As we experience more, and as our understanding grows, our energies change. And consequently, two people who fell in love and who initially "clicked" on five levels might find themselves, several or many years later, with only one or two common flows—enough to still care about each other, but not enough to really bond them closely anymore.

This can be very confusing and embarrassing for everyone involved, and it helps explain why long-standing and seemingly perfect relationships suddenly break up for no apparent reason. The underlying reason is that energy, like water, continually seeks its own level. When that level cannot be found with the main person in one's life, it is sought elsewhere, in other people or activities. Again, just like the initial finding of rapport, this new searching often takes place unconsciously.

Many people have difficulty accepting growth or change, whether it is their own or someone else's. Those who were raised with a "till death do us part" ethic find these moments especially troublesome. Some attempt to avoid them by pretending that nothing has changed, while shifting most of their time and attention to the grandchildren or various church or charity interests or new hobbies. Energies which cannot be shared in these contexts may become dammed up within the individual, and can cause a multitude of dis-eases, ranging from simple to serious.

Keeping an old relationship, and filling in the cracks with new activities, may prevent divorce or social displacement, but it also prohibits the finding of another individual with whom one could grow and share again. Some people, indeed, are too frightened or too skeptical to try again. But there are no guarantees in life. Everything is a gamble. Everything changes. And a relationship which one or two people have outgrown is not a failure—anything which has helped one grow, however minutely, or however painfully, is still a success. First grade was not a failure. It was preparation for what followed: second grade.

We need to be very careful in dealing with people, to understand that change can be painful, and even abrupt. Yet growth is right, even when it occasionally causes us great upheavals and discomfort.

And there is another factor to be considered here. In good, constructive human relationships, each person remains independent and cultivates his or her own growth at all levels of being. One becomes responsible for oneself and one's actions. This leads to strength and understanding which can be shared in all relationships—business, social, or personal.

What often happens, however, is that people get stuck; they reach a point where they feel that they cannot handle their lives or relationships and they attempt to abdicate responsibility. Such a person expresses "poor me" or "woe is me!" sentiments, hoping that others will take pity and not expect the poor thing to resume responsibility. Poor thing becomes a "leaner" and will lean on anyone who allows this behavior to continue—boss, spouse, friends, children, parents. The unfortunate part is that leaning is escaping, and only serves to make one weaker; while every attempt to accept responsibility and live more constructively and make wiser choices strengthens a person.

It is interesting that we do not allow leaners (crybabies) in sports, but we feel sorry for them in our personal lives. In sports, we expect an athlete who has just lost a game or event to re-evaluate the game plan and then practice and prepare for the next competition. That same attitude can apply in all aspects of life.

Cording

If you live or work with any leaners, and if they consider you stronger than themselves, you can rest assured that they have helped themselves to some of the energy in your aura. They do this by a process known as "cording." Clairvoyants can see these cords of energy between people. A cord can also be used to send energy to someone else's chakra, but that isn't advisable, either. In both cases, you are furnishing energy (with or without your consent) which the other person needs to learn to generate for himself or herself. It is much better, all along the way, for you to keep your own energy and let the other person keep his or hers. You can mix auras without trading energy, or at least without grasping any.

Cords can originate whenever two people share a common belief. Cords attach at the appropriate chakra relating to the belief. It is a good idea to re-evaluate all your relationships periodically. Are you and the other person both strong? Have one or both of you inadvertently been leaning on the other? Would your life continue on basically the same if this person were no longer on the scene? Could you survive without the other person? Would you want to? Anytime that you don't hold all the keys to your own life, you have given away some of your power. Remember, you want to be a strong person sharing from your position of strength; you do not want to be a person who is growing continuously weaker because you have given away your strength.

One irony of all this is that no amount of assistance from outside will ever strengthen a weak person. Strength must be developed internally as a consequence of action. Swimming with the tide (floating, inertia) does not develop muscles; taking action in one's life strengthens one for further action.

Where should you look for cords? Here is a listing, giving the cords most commonly associated with each of the major chakras.

1. *Base Chakra.*   Ideas about survival. Primary desire. Material or spiritual desires: anything that you let control you. Anything you must have to survive. Anything that drives you.

2. *Spleen Chakra.*   Ideas about sexuality and reproduction. Sexual attraction. How you feel about any demands on your sexual or emotional attention. How you feel about body types ("skinny," neutral, "fat"). Balance, especially on mental levels. Soul.

3. *Solar Plexus Chakra.*   All emotions. Emotions relating to power. Power-trips. Marriage. Work. Energy. Emotions affect everything and are related to the mind.

4. *Heart Chakra.*   Concepts about love. Whatever it takes to provide you with security. Feelings of esteem, at any point on the continuum from joyful and happy to sad and depressed. Self-worth. Self-pity.

5. *Throat Chakra.*   Expression of the feelings. How you feel about expressing your feelings. Creativity (non-physical). Will. Free-will. Communication. Knowing and speaking your truth (what you know to be true, despite what others or the culture or religions say).

6. *Eye Chakra (Ajna).*   Seeing things eye to eye. Strong thinking between people. Ideals, beliefs. Openmindedness, or closedmindedness. Willfulness. Judgmental. Christ consciousness. Intuitive seeing.

7. *Crown Chakra.*   Your conception of the Creative Force. Religion. Universal consciousness. Control. Intuitive knowing.

If you think or know that cords exist between you and someone else, you can use the following exercise to remove them.

PERFECT FREEDOM EXERCISE (UNCORDING)

Sit in a comfortable position with your back straight. Close your eyes and take three deep breaths. Inhale slowly through the nose and exhale fully.

In your imagination, travel to a seaport. Find yourself walking along a pier, toward a ship that is coming in to dock. See the passengers waving at you.

Pay careful attention to the passengers as you get closer to them. Do an uncording with the first person you see who is familiar to you.

(1) Begin with the base chakra. You can picture the cords as being the same colors as the chakras. This one is red. See the cord as a rope. Untie the rope that has been placed around yourself at the level of the base of the spine, and be careful to seal the hole where the cord comes out of your chakra. Then remove the other end of the cord from the other person, again being sure to seal the hole in the chakra. Toss the loosened cord into the ocean and watch it disappear. With the removal of each cord, you should feel more balanced.

(2) Proceed to the next chakra, the navel, which is orange in color. Visualize the removal as before, and the sealing up, and the tossing away of the cord. Picture all of this as vividly as you can.

(3) Go to the solar plexus chakra (yellow), at the tip of your breastbone. Remove and toss away the cord as before.

(4) Then go to the heart center (green), at the top of the breast-bone, and follow the same procedure.

(5) Next move to the throat chakra, at the level of the Adam's apple. This chakra is blue.

(6) The sixth chakra, the ajna, is located between the eyes, and its color is indigo.

(7) The final chakra, the crown, is located at the top of the head, and the color is violet.

Once all the cords have been removed, picture yourself as strong and whole and surrounded with the pink light of Universal health and love. Then picture the other person as strong and whole and surrounded in pink. Mentally tell the other person: "I choose perfect freedom. I give you perfect freedom. May your life be blessed. Go in peace."

As that person returns to the ship, another passenger may come forward. Even deceased people may present themselves to you. Uncord with all of them in the same fashion.

After you have finished with the people who have come forward, look closely at the passengers still on deck. There may be a cluster of people whom you know. If so, do a group uncording with them. Remove each cord from yourself and then from the corresponding chakra of the entire group. Bless the group before they depart.

Take three deep breaths, come back to present time, and note how you feel. You may want to record the date, those who came forward, and how you felt about each person before and after the uncording. This exercise can bring to the surface very powerful feelings or attitudes which you have not noticed before.

Pay very special attention to your relationships with all those people from now on. You will notice subtle and not-so-subtle changes in the relationships. As you become stronger, you will also become more sensitive to interpersonal impacts.

Make a date with yourself to re-examine this first information after a week has passed. If you feel that you have changed, but that someone else is resistant to allowing you perfect freedom, do the uncording exercise with that person daily. Ask that the other person be blessed with love and understanding so that both of you can go forward toward growth.

Uncording will help you understand your own past behavior and will give you insights into how you have chosen or evaluated others. You may, in fact, discover that you initially invited the cording. (Being needed by someone else gives you power and perhaps self-satisfaction.) Now you have the option of choosing freedom for yourself and others in all interactions.

PROTECTING YOUR ENERGY FIELD

We are all constantly mixing auras with others. And we need to be careful in order to maintain the purity of our auras. While we can never isolate ourselves from others, we can take steps to protect ourselves from unwanted influences. Here are some simple methods that work.

To Protect the Aura

1. Cross your arms in front of you.

2. Interlace your hands behind you.

3. Stand with your weight on your left foot.

4. See a whirlwind of white energy coming into your aura and taking all extraneous materials down into the Earth.

5. Imagine the "pores" of your aura opening wider and letting the information from the other person pass right on through.

6. Imagine yourself clothed in a robe of white light.

7

TOUCH

Touching is one of the things which Nature wants us to do. She is so insistent about it that touch for humans is like sunshine for plants. With the right amount, we flower and prosper; with too little, we never achieve full growth; with too much, we become burnt out or burned up before our time.

The right amount of touch, though, may be an individual matter. It may also be considerably more than many of us have been getting, because recent research has proven that there are many health benefits to touch. There are also human or societal benefits.

Touch at its best can be an expression of love and concern which is a blessing both to the giver and to the receiver. As an expression of the highest emotions we can imagine, touch can even be spiritual or Divine.

There are many levels and kinds of touch. Touch can be light or deep, fast or slow, and of short or long duration. Touch can be social, friendly, professional, intimate, caring, therapeutic, familial, disciplinary, sexual, aggressive, or violent. The meaning of the touch is more important than the actual physical touch. Certainly, we all recognize quickly a touch which is meant to punish or harm us, and our immediate instinct is to get away. So it is not touching that produces positive results, but harmless touching.

In using touch to help others heal themselves, we must go a step further: we must convey not only our own harmless intent, but also our commitment to helpfulness.

Many people have difficulty touching their own bodies or any one else's, because of past societal emphasis on touch as a vehicle for sex and punishment. Some people are therefore suspicious of those who touch them, or of anyone who touches someone beyond the perfunctory handshake.

TYPES AND TECHNIQUES OF TOUCH

It would be good for all of us to go back to the beginning and to re-examine the types and techniques of touch that we use in all of our dealings with others.

1. *Social.*   From the simple handshake to an embrace to a full-bodied hug, and maybe even a kiss. The meaning may be, "Here we are in the same place. I'm having a good time. I'm glad you're here, and I hope you're having a good time, too." This may be a business meeting, a wedding, or a graduation, and the interaction can be with a friend, an acquaintance, or a stranger, depending upon the openness of the people involved.

2. *Friendly.*   This can cover many forms of touch, depending upon the the two people involved. It conveys, "I care about you. You're special or important to me, and I'm glad we're friends." The level of touch may change over time, and it usually reaches an unspoken agreement between the two (with each one assuming that the other's degree of openness has established the level at which s/he feels comfortable).

3. *Professional.*   The way the doctor or dentist touches—partly to comfort, partly to carry out the examination or proce-dure. This acknowledges you as a person, but means nothing after-ward. The professional is interested in your comfort because you

are a client, but s/he has no particular interest in you personally. The touch is merely part of a diagnostic routine. This would also include the touch of the nurse, nurse's aide, orderly, dietitian, or any other personnel attending to patients in a clinic or hospital setting. Touching you is incidental to doing their job.

Some teachers touch in this way, also. With teachers, however, it is more problematic, because teachers spend a good deal of time with pupils, and unless the pupils are adults, there may be confusion about the teacher's meaning and intent.

4. *Intimate.* This is the kind of touch about which most of us dream. [There are a few non-tactile types around who simply don't want or need intimate touch . . . or, more likely, who have not yet realized how fulfilling and healing joyous touch can be.] Touch here is extremely personal—whether its intention is to lead onward to sexuality or not.

Intimate touch is reserved for the closest of friends, or a spouse or a mate. This is the touch of someone you know deeply and whom you also touch, the touch of those who mean the most to you as a complete person.

Other touches fall into categories; here, the categories are transcended. The two of you are allowed and encouraged to touch each other openly at all times. This presupposes an open communication between the two people. Failure to communicate—or to comprehend what is communicated—will result in less intimacy. This, too, is conveyed in the touch (or lack of touch, or change in touch), although it is not always sensed or acted upon.

Nothing stays the same: intimacy levels rise or fall, depending upon the state of the whole relationship. Intimacy levels can, however, like all else in the Universe, be cyclic. The point to note is that if shared communication gradually falls below what one partner considers to be an acceptable level, their intimacy factor will also be affected. Sometimes, when both people value the relationship and want it to continue at a deep level, they can discuss everything freely and fully and restore (or even increase) the intimacy factor. If, however, the two people cannot agree on one or more important aspects of the relationship, the intimacy factor will almost certainly decrease. The relationship may continue, and may even be helpful to both individuals, but the relationship and the intimacy of it have changed.

Once this occurs, neither person can achieve full growth in that relationship. Each may pursue private interests, and look to friends or groups for the satisfaction that cannot be gained in the intimate relationship. People often turn to business, or family, or religious or fraternal groups for a feeling of total acceptance and understanding. In none of these settings is one expected to be, or confronted with the necessity to be, intimate.

Many people, in fact, think intimacy is automatic. It is not. Like most other human behavior, it is learned. And it takes *practice*. This is one reason why so many second or third marriages succeed. Once we know enough to be able to start making mature decisions, we begin to choose our intimate relationships more carefully. Perhaps, too, we grow less selfish and more appreciative of compassionate others as our maturity deepens.

5. *Caring.* This type can really be found in any setting, among any grouping of people. It can be the mother or father comforting the child. It can be a stranger in an airport offering comfort to another passenger traveling to attend a loved one's funeral. It can be two co-workers congratulating each other after the company has decided to adopt their advertising campaign. Here, the touch means, "I am one human reaching out to another, on the basis of our shared humanity." This touch, perhaps more than others, recognizes that humans are unique. We feel, we plan. And we know that others do the same. Reaching out acknowledges that we are all in this together, and that we can appreciate the joy or sorrow in the other person's life.

6. *Therapeutic.* Categories here include massage and other forms of healing which utilize touch methods. This differs from the diagnostic touch used by professionals, although professional therapists may do the touching here. Therefore, all healing touch can rightfully be considered therapeutic. Physical therapists, occupational therapists, nurses, massage therapists, and athletic team trainers fall into this description. Touching you is a way of helping your body toward healing and wholeness. The touch is, and should be, impersonal. This is why professionals do not treat their families or friends. Healers may be an exception. Some healers do very well with people they know; others do not.

7. *Familial/Clan.* Touch here occurs because of birth or marriage. Touch among family members is considered healthy. Touch which affirms the whole personhood of another is healthy. We are discovering that much more care must occur here, in order to help children have all the benefits of positive touch and to teach them to protect themselves from negative touching (invasive touch). Touch within the family is good if it leads to full expression and well-rounded development outside the family as well. Some people become habituated to their family to such an extent that they never relate openly or fully to anyone outside the family (including their spouses and their own children). This can occur even without any touching, and may be nearly as harmful as actual physical incest, in that all following relationships (personal and social) are inhibited even before their inception.

Good family touching is comforting and rewarding for parents, children, siblings, grandparents, and other relatives. Trans-generational touching gives people a sense of their beginnings, their roots, and even an understanding of what they may look like and be like when they are older. Just as grandparents transcend the parents in age (and, perhaps, in growth and understanding), so do the society, the nation, and the planet, each transcend the family.

What one learns here, one can apply elsewhere. What enriches here, will enrich the world. To stifle a child is to prevent the planet from knowing full growth.

Touching here means that you are good, lovable, acceptable, and worthy, just because you are a human being. Every human has the right to know and to feel these basic acceptances. These are givens; they are not earned. Wise parents teach children how to act responsibly and respectfully. Such a child can thereby earn respect and recognition from others through his or her work, actions, and behaviors. In this way, the child can build his or her own life constructively. New methods and new attention given to these basic foundations of personhood will make greater achievement possible for each future generation.

8. *Disciplining.* This may occur at home, at school, or elsewhere. Some may be preventive or protective—holding a child's hand while waiting for the light to turn green. The purpose of discipline is to instill correct behavior. Useful methods do this by encouraging the child to understand why a certain behavior is encouraged or desired over other behaviors. By taking a positive approach, discipline becomes an educational rather than a punitive tool. Some people believe that discipline should never involve hitting a child, and they are probably correct. Hitting is usually a reflection of an adult's anger and frustration. Some children respect hitting, and others seem oblivious to it. Consequently, it is probably the better part of wisdom to get a child's attention with a disciplining touch, and then to offer a better suggestion for adopting appropriate behaviors.

Young children have no concept of right or wrong, so trying to convince them to "be good" is futile. I even suspect that young children see their parents' auras and are fascinated by them, and that the children try out a range of behaviors to see what effect each behavior will have on the parental auras. Be clever. Try to discover positive ways to teach and reinforce good behaviors. If you reward yourself for finishing adult projects, reward your child for doing things correctly. Rewards can be small and can be time spent together, rather than expensive gifts or toys.

9. *Sexual.*   While most sexual touch falls into the category of intimate touch, there are some for whom sexuality can occur on a non-intimate basis. In fact, new research has shown that many of us find it easier to be sexual than to be intimate, even with those closest to us. Perhaps this merely shows that we have a stronger drive to be sexual than we do to be intimate, at least in the present cultural climate. One hopes this will change. Just because it is easier to be sexual does not mean that it is preferable to be sexual than to be intimate. In fact, I would guess that anyone who has learned to be intimate would always prefer an intimate relationship to a plain old sexual encounter.

NEGATIVE, OR INVASIVE, TOUCH

10. *Aggressive or Unwanted Sexual.*   This is unwanted caressing, fondling, molestation [rape by a known person]. It is clearly invasive of the dignity and the innate divinity of the victim, and it violates the personhood as well as the physical body of the one being attacked. This is not a harmless touch; it is selfish touching, and it has negative impacts on both individuals. Where an adult seduces or attacks a child, the adult in fact mutilates the child's sense of trust and beingness. The child knows this is wrong behavior, but because the child does not have an adult value system, the child cannot evaluate the behavior from an adult understanding. The child almost always internalizes the experience to mean, "If this could happen to me, I must be bad, wrong, horrible, and unlovable."

As the child grows to adulthood, he or she may or may not evaluate these childhood happenings in a more realistic and constructive way. It is always difficult for such children to develop trust—in themselves or in others. Left unexamined and unresolved these early feelings are turned into, "I am bad, and so I'll act bad." They thus become the basis for using others, destroying oneself (through drugs, alcohol, or suicide), or destroying others, by battering or abusing spouses and children when the now-adult encounters frustrations. Clearly, every invasive act has far-reaching consequences.

11. *Violent Touch, Sadistic Touch, Rape.*   This is full-blown aggression, which may be born of something in the perpetrator's past, and is thereby "excused" by himself or herself in an attempt to get even with a person or the Universe.

The purpose of touch here is to hurt, to cause pain, to force another to comply with one's selfish wishes. This is the polar opposite of love, compassion, and sympathy.

Such acts can only be committed by those filled with pain and hatred—which are merely love turned inside out; love, in fact, unreturned, unrequited, *untouched.*

The sooner we can eliminate types 10 and 11 from our touch categories, the better. One of the best ways to do this is to begin touching each other more now in all settings. Many of us are hungry for touch and do not even realize it. It is our hunger for touch that makes us evaluate every touch from another person. If we were comfortable with touching, we would be glad for good touches and would know how to give "thanks, anyway," messages to unwelcome approaches. We wouldn't have to wonder why someone touched us, as we do now, every time someone new touches us or every time someone we know touches us in a new and different way.

Touch is much more than a means of sharing or communicating. It is apparently vital to our physical development and to our mental health at all ages.

Premature babies given extra periods of touch grow faster than they would otherwise. Normal babies given enough touch may crawl, walk, and talk earlier, and may also develop more intelligence than normal children who receive only an ordinary amount of touch. If you're feeling down, and someone cuddles you, your body discharges a new chemical which can make you feel better in one-millionth of a second. Touch, indeed, stimulates the production of many chemicals in the brain which affect our body's cells. A body deprived of touch might as well be a body deprived of food.

And, when we are happy, the pleasure centers in our brains are turned on and the pain centers are turned off. This is why laughter or a positive frame of mind lessen pain, while depression or self-pity intensify pain sensations. Impulses of pleasure or pain trigger the manufacture of chemicals in the brain which combine with hormones and enzymes in the blood to produce moods and feelings. In a sense, then, positive touching can create a real chemical high in the body.

Touching actually speeds recuperation and is very good for the sick or grieving. As we begin to use touch for these purposes, though, it is wise to establish some definite guidelines.

HEALING, HARMLESS TOUCH

Touching, to ease pain or hasten healing, should always convey at least two elements:

1) Your level of awareness regarding the importance and place of touch in the healing process; and

2) Your comprehension of the other person's feelings and concerns both in regard to the problem at hand and as a whole person.

A third element can also be expressed:
3) Touch as a channel to convey healing or spiritual energies.

It is important for you to distinguish these things in order to concentrate on this specialized form of touch and its appropriate uses. While you recognize the complete person before you, you want to focus your attention on the positive, beneficial results of the healing touch. It is probably wise to draw upon aspects of both *professional* and *therapeutic* touch, as described earlier, to devise an impersonally-personal approach in dealing with others.

Be careful in touching.   In employing any healing method, you are merely assisting the other person in bringing his or her body back to a state of normalcy so that it can heal itself in the present and maintain health into the future. Therefore, the relationship between you, in such a setting, should be impersonal. You want the person to learn to become stronger and more able to become whole. You do not want the person to become reliant upon or dependent upon you. You want the person to discover and become the independent and strong individual residing inside him or her.

Teach others by your example to become whole, complete, healthy, caring individuals. Once the person is whole and is able to accept responsibility for his or her present and future well-being, the two of you, as whole and independent individuals, may freely choose whatever level and degree of interaction seems appropriate and comfortable to both of you.

8

MUSCLE-TESTING

Applied Kinesiology (or muscle-testing) has shown that everything in and around the body either strengthens or weakens the energy field. Muscle-testing is simple to do, but it does require two people.

Have your friend or relative stand up straight, with the left arm relaxed at the side of the body. The right arm is held straight out, at shoulder level, on the side of the body.

Face the person and place your right hand on the left shoulder to steady him or her. Now place your left hand just above the person's right wrist. Explain that you will try to push the arm down as he or she resists. Push down quickly and firmly. Be gentle in doing this. You are testing the ability of the muscle to lock the shoulder joint momentarily. You are not trying to find out which of you is stronger, or how long the muscle can resist. All you need is the initial reaction of strength or weakness.

In most cases, your partner will be able to resist this initial pressure. Then perform the test a second time while your partner eats candy, has a plastic bag resting on the top of his or her head, or thinks of an unhappy moment. Almost always, the formerly strong muscle immediately becomes weak.

What happened? Something temporarily interrupted the body's energy flow. It can be an internal or external event—or even a thought or a feeling.

You can use muscle-testing to change your environment into

one which provides an energy-enhancing "diet" for you. You can test clothing, food, nutrients (vitamin and mineral supplements), herbs, medicines, emotions, thoughts, and any objects or materials at home or in any other workplace. Some materials (cotton and other natural fibers) are universally strengthening, while others always weaken the energy field (refined sugar, plastic). The response to other items is unique to the individual. I often test to see which brand of same-potency vitamin or mineral supplement a given body prefers.

To test substances, first do the muscle test outlined above. If the muscle is strong, continue on. If the muscle tests weak, tap the thymus (behind the top of the breastbone) three or four times. Then place the substance you want to test in your mouth (food, medicine, or supplement) or at your thymus. Hold it at the thymus while someone re-tests the muscle for you. Go by what your body tells you. If the muscle has been weakened, avoid this item. If you have any doubts about the validity of the test results, repeat the tests several times on different occasions until you are convinced that the results are accurate.

Then, if you choose to do so, you can use this new knowledge to make immediate changes in your life which will strengthen your field. This makes more energy available to you on all levels. It is rather like plugging the holes in a sieve (although the results will be more subtle): it is hard to realize how much energy you have been losing until you get used to having it again. You may notice an immediate increase in your energy level. Some people feel more alert, more even-tempered, or considerably less stressed than before.

It is important to respect the physical body—via diet, exercise, and energy—because it is the agent through which we express our emotions, our thoughts, our ideas; without the physical, we cannot speak or hear or write, or act or build or worship on an external level. Anything which strengthens the energy field makes it easier for the physical body to remain healthy and become a willing vehicle through which the non-physical aspects of ourselves can gain expression.

Another important lesson which muscle-testing teaches is that "thinking makes it so." You may not be able to control events, but you can always choose how you will respond to them. Positive reactions strengthen the body; negative reactions weaken it. That is why we have always been advised to "look on the bright side of things" and to count our blessings. It is not so much events that shape us, as it is our reactions to them. We can forever lament one missed promotion, or we can implement ten improvements in our own performance in our present position, while developing all the necessary skills so that there will be no doubt, next time, about who deserves an opportunity for advancement. The lesson is clear. We can *choose* health by taking responsibility for our thoughts, feelings, and actions, and by learning to focus on the good in all things—especially when that good is not self-evident.

ENERGY-FIELD STRENGTHENERS

1. Thump your thymus (behind the top of the breastbone).

2. Sit upright.

3. Smile.

4. Think of positive emotions (love) or virtues (peace, patience, faith, hope, contentment).

For a more complete introduction to muscle-testing for the lay-person, see *Your Body Doesn't Lie*, by John Diamond, M.D., which is available in paperback.

9

POLARITY

Polarity Therapy is a system which was designed by Randolph Stone, who was born in Austria in 1890 and emigrated to the United States at age 13. He studied many methods of healing and earned doctoral degrees in osteopathy, chiropractic, and naturopathy. He traveled extensively and became familiar with Shiatsu, yoga, acupuncture, and the Hermetic, Caballistic, and Ayurvedic healing traditions. Stone synthesized much of his learning as he developed Polarity Therapy. He retired in 1973, moving to India, after sixty years of practice and teaching. Dr. Pierre Pannetier was selected by Stone to become his successor.

Polarity is based upon the fact that the body is a magnet, and, like a bar magnet, is surrounded by an electromagnetic field.

Energy must flow freely through this field in order for health to be maintained. Stress can interrupt the flow of electrical current; and if these short circuits continue, illness will eventually manifest in the physical body. Clairvoyants can see disease-potentials in the aura six months prior to any physical manifestation.

The purpose of a polarity session is to strengthen an already healthy electromagnetic field, and, where short circuits, or energy blockages, have occurred, to restore and re-polarize the energy so that it will again be flowing freely in the correct direction. Once that has been accomplished, the correct flow can be continued and strengthened by proper exercise, attitude, and diet. Thus the long-term responsibility for well-being rests with the individual. [See chapters on *Exercise* and *Affirmation*.]

Polarity is easy to learn and to use. It is always beneficial, although if you are a strongly energized person who is working on a child or a frail or a severely injured adult, you must be careful not to overwhelm your recipient with energy. Polarity is—or should be—a *gentle* means of assisting the body so that it may heal itself.

EXPERIENCING ENERGY

Rub your hands together vigorously for thirty seconds. Then hold your hands apart, facing each other. Move the hands closer together and then up to six inches apart, several times. Note any sensations of cold, warmth, tingling, or vibrating.

Now clap your hands for twenty seconds, and again try to feel the energy in each hand and the flow of energy back and forth between your hands. You are feeling the flow of electromagnetic energy. Rubbing or clapping stimulates both the flow and the awareness of your nerves to the passage of energy through them.

You can use this energy to aid yourself or others.

ENERGY FLOW

The basic flow of energy in the body is from North [head, (+), positive] to South [feet, (–), negative]. Just as in a magnet, however, there is a neutral [(0)] field where both forces [(+) and (–)] are balanced.

The energy must, in fact, change polarity in order to flow from one part of the field to the next. And if the energy becomes blocked at *any* level, then everything above and below the blockage will also be affected by the interruption of the normal flow. Therefore, it is vitally important for health that the energy be able to move.

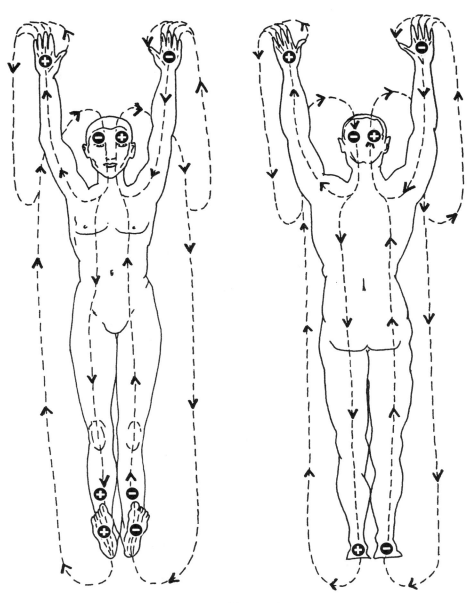

FIGURE 1

This electromagnetic field around the body is more commonly known as the human *aura*. The innermost part of the aura inter-penetrates the physical body and also extends up to one-half inch beyond it. This segment has also been called the *physical aura* or the *etheric body*. Other sections of the aura fan out from the body and can extend as far as twenty feet in developed persons. Different layers of the aura relate to different energy levels: emotional, mental, and spiritual. Gifted clairvoyants can "read" a person's level of development through the aura.

The actual flow of energy in and around the physical body is somewhat more intricate: energy runs *down* the front right side of the body and *up* the back right side. Energy runs *up* the left front side of the body and *down* the back left side. (See Fig. 1)

Please note that the designation of any section as positive (+), negative (–), or neutral (0) is *relative*, because the flow makes an area seem to have a particular polarity, yet all three forces [(+), (–), (0)] are always present everywhere: what changes is which force is predominant in a given location.

Each segment of the body can be further broken up into smaller magnets (Fig. 2). The entire body can be depicted in this fashion. (Fig. 3)

It is important to understand this roadmap of the body in order to derive full benefit from polarity, because the body can and does transfer messages from one place to another. If you energize any positive (+) site on the body, this input is immediately and automatically transmitted to every other like-poled (+) site on the body.

This has two pertinent applications. The first is that if someone has a broken ankle, you can give energy through the other ankle or both wrists and other similar-poled sites. If someone is burned over a large portion of the body, you can work with whatever sections are left unburned. (Or, even better, you can always work one-half inch away from the body, which achieves the same results as touching the body.)

Secondly, your body and your subconscious mind always try to help you stay functional. So a nagging pain in your back may not be caused by poor posture, but rather by the nasty whack which you got on your right forearm a few months ago. Healing can be reflexed throughout the body, and so can discomfort. Such transfers are not always readily apparent; suspect them whenever the simple treatment of a symptom does not bring relief.

[CAUTION: DIAGNOSIS IS AN ART, AND THE ABILITY OF THE BODY TO REFLEX MAKES DIAGNOSIS EVEN MORE CHALLENGING. DO NOT ATTEMPT TO DIAGNOSE YOURSELF OR OTHERS UNLESS YOU ARE A QUALIFIED MEMBER OF THE MEDICAL PROFESSION.]

Reflexing enables you to assist the whole body through one hand or foot, when necessary or convenient. I often use the feet as a miniature map of the body which enables me to quickly locate any blockages. I then use polarity to dissolve the blocks. [Study the chapter on *Reflexology* for related ideas.]

FIGURE 2

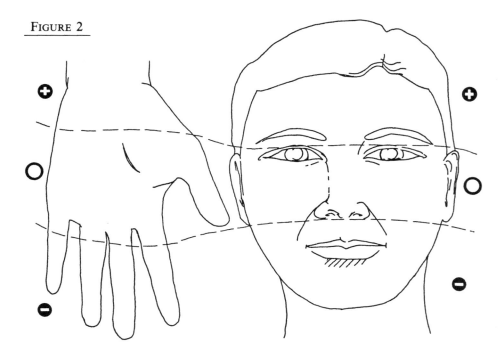

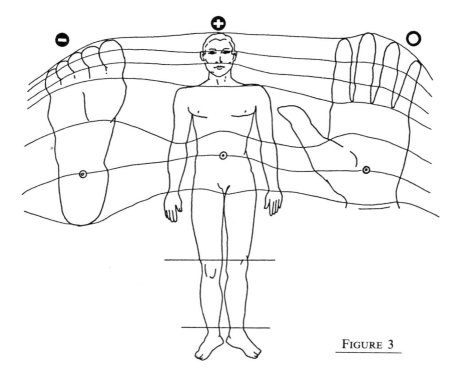

FIGURE 3

THE HANDS

The palm of each hand contains an energy chakra, so whenever you place your palms on the body, you create a line of energy between them. The right hand is generally designated as the positive (+) hand and the left hand as the negative (−). For this reason, you usually stand to the right of the person you're working on, because opposites attract, and the top of the body (+) will accept the energy from the left hand (−) more readily. (Fig. 4)

Each digit of the hand also has a particular charge: the thumbs are neutral (0); the forefingers are negative (−); the middlefingers are positive (+); the ring fingers are negative (−); and the little fingers are positive (+). The left forefinger has the maximum negative (−) charge, and the right middlefinger has the maximum

FIGURE 4

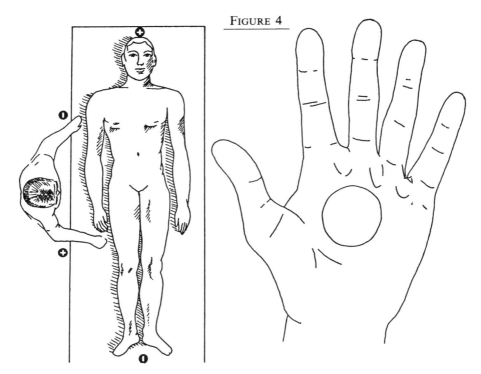

positive (+) charge. (Fig. 5) Consequently, these two fingers can be used in place of the two palms.

Actually, the energy is going to flow no matter what you do. You can stand on the left side of the person and use any combination of fingers, palms, or thumbs, and the energy will still flow. The polarity of the energy changes over at so many sites on the body (chakras, mid-lines on front and back of the body, every joint) that the correct flow will be established if you begin the session by putting the poles back in place (as will be described later).

Practice on both sides of the body, because it is fun (and therapeutic) for two or more people to give a session to another person, and you will want to be familiar with holds applied from all positions around the body.

It is also good to practice sending energy through the arms and legs, from side to side, and top to bottom. (Fig. 6) Picture laser-

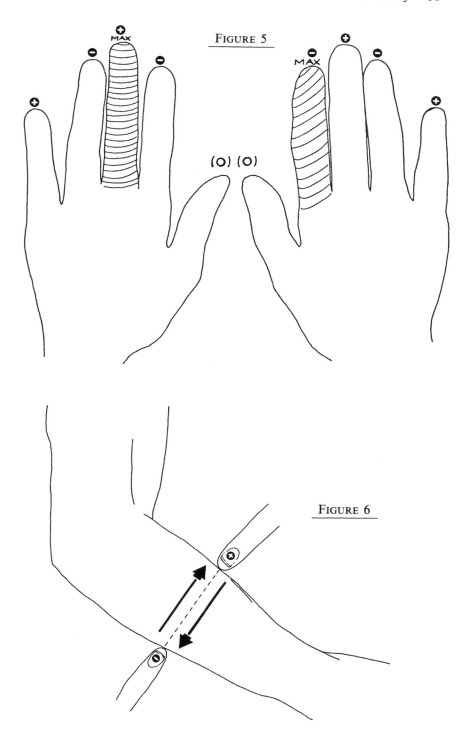

FIGURE 5

(O) (O)

FIGURE 6

like streams of energy coming from the fingertips of both hands. With more practice, you will be able to send this energy through the body, too. I prefer to use this method, rather than massage, to help relax sore muscles. I visualize the energy from my fingertips melting the blockage away. This is faster than massage and creates no further pain or congestion in the body.

Switchboards

The body has four switchboards which can receive or send energy [(+), (–), (0)] as needed. Energy may be channeled from a switchboard to any other point on the body, including a second switchboard. In fact, some of the most powerful holds are between switchboards. They are found at the navel, the coccyx (very base of the spine), the occiput (base of the skull), and the frontal eminence (center of the highest part of the forehead). (Fig. 7)

You can use switchboards to help others, but they are also excellent to use for self-treatment, either for the relief of pain, or for general energizing. To relieve pain, hold one hand on any switchboard, and the other hand over the site of pain. Use your hand to pull the blockage out of the aura and throw it away. Once the pain has subsided, hold the site on the body, and picture energy running between your hands to re-establish the normal flow.

Switchboards can be used to detect and remedy weak spots in the etheric. Hold the navel with the right palm and use the left palm to slowly sweep over the upper body. This takes practice. If you find a temperature difference, visualize energy from your left palm warming the area to match the rest of the area. Then move on. Once the upper body has been covered, put your left hand on the navel and use your right hand to feel the aura over the lower body.

There is one caution here: avoid the coccyx on people prone to epilepsy or on those with very high blood pressure.

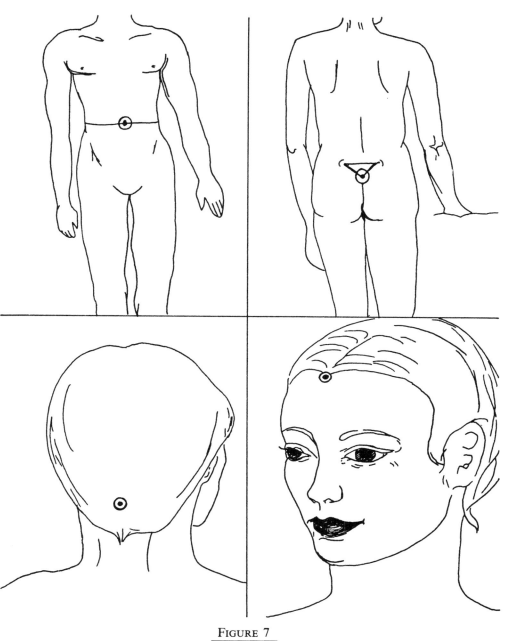

FIGURE 7

Rules for Polarity

1. Polarity will work on infants, animals, skeptics, and everyone else. In the beginning, however, you will find that the less you talk, the better, so that you can concentrate.

2. If you and your partner can both visualize the energy, the two of you will accomplish more. Two minds in agreement multiply results.

3. Always observe your partner, to make sure s/he is comfortable. If for any reason your partner becomes uncomfortable, stop immediately. In rare instances, a healing crisis may occur, which will intensify the person's symptoms. Be alert and aware. Calm your partner. Then immediately wash your hands in cold water. This removes any extraneous energy which you may have picked up from your partner's aura.

4. Make the environment conducive to healing. You want the session to be peaceful and uninterrupted. Unplug the telephones. Quiet, meditative music is all right, although some people prefer silence.

5. It is not necessary to have any equipment. You can work on people in any position. However, if you are serious about polarity, you will eventually want a massage table. This saves your back and legs and also affords your partner maximum relaxation on a comfortable surface.

6. Wear comfortable clothing. I prefer loose-fitting lightweight cotton. Some people work barefooted.

7. Remove all possible metal from your partner and yourself. Take off jewelry, belt buckles, eyeglasses. Empty pockets. Your partner may want to remove contact lenses.

8. Ask your partner what s/he is feeling, energy-wise, as the session progresses. Your own observations may not be telling you enough. Results may not be immediately apparent, either; but in any event, you need to stay in rapport with your partner so that you understand how s/he is experiencing the session. If the partner senses that the two of you are out of communication, s/he can create a mental blockage which will prevent the free flow of energy.

9. Responses may vary from sleep all the way up to blissful ecstasy. It all depends upon your partner. Time perceptions are usually altered; an hour-long session may have only seemed like fifteen minutes to your partner.

10. Sessions may be given as often as necessary. Several per day may be used in acute conditions (burns, wounds, fractures, sprains, pain) *if the person is basically healthy*. Serious and chronic conditions respond better to sessions every other day. These are ideals. Benefits will still be obtained even if sessions cannot be given this frequently. However, long sessions are more taxing on the body. Older or frail people should have frequent, shorter sessions.

11. In order for real healing to occur, your partner must be willing to exercise, think, and eat in health-promoting ways. This begins with taking responsibility for oneself in every aspect of life.

12. Children respond well, and with their smaller bodies, a little energy goes a long way. Animals, too, are usually smaller and should be given shorter sessions.

13. Using a few holds well is more beneficial than hurrying through every hold you know. Adjust the session to meet the needs of the partner, letting your intuition guide you.

14. Give sessions only to people you like. Refer others to professionals.

15. Make sure everyone's expectations are realistic. Instantaneous healings do occur, but rarely.

16. Give sessions only when you feel healthy and balanced yourself.

17. Avoid injured and infected areas, and never apply pressure to internal organs. You want to alleviate pain, not cause it.

18. Do not claim to treat, give therapy, or heal. Do not diagnose or prescribe, because these are the legal provinces of the medical profession.

You may, if you wish, give polarity sessions for research, educational, or recreational purposes, or as part of your religion.

The Polarity Session

Have your partner remove shoes and hosiery and lie down on his or her back. If a massage table is not available, any flat surface may be used. Whenever possible, have your partner place his or her head to the North and feet to the South. This aligns him or her with the Earth's polarity.

Explain that your partner's only task is to breathe deeply, relax, and enjoy the session. Practice deep breathing together several times: inhale noisily through the nose and sigh a big sigh of relief as you exhale through the mouth. This will help both of you to relax. Tension impedes the energy, so do all you can to stay relaxed. If you note your partner tensing up during the session, repeat the breathing-together until your partner relaxes.

You and your partner can be as quiet or as talkative as you want, but try to keep distractions of all kinds at a minimum.

Begin by centering yourself. See yourself grounded to the center of the Earth by a golden cord coming from the base of your spine.

FIGURE 8

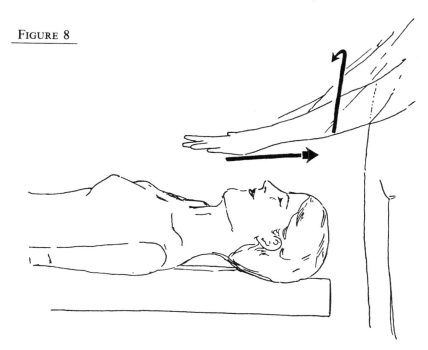

Then see energy from the Sun entering your body through your crown chakra. See this Solar energy filling your entire aura. Then ask your partner to see himself or herself grounded to the center of the Earth by a golden cord emerging from the end of the spine. (Visualize this vividly yourself as you describe it to your partner.) Then invite the partner to see himself or herself surrounded by the healing energies of the Universe. (You can suggest the Solar energy you've used on yourself.)

1) *Cleansing the Field*

Stand at the top of the table, with your abdomen facing your partner's head. Stretch your fingers and, without touching the body, "wipe off" the extraneous energy three inches from the partner's head. Start at the neck and move upward and off the head. (Fig. 8) Fling this stale energy out into an empty space near-by. Wipe off and fling the energy away two more times.

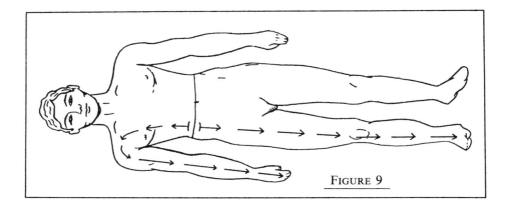

Figure 9

Move around the table to your right, and stand at the waist on the right side of the body. Starting with your hands at the waist, again a few inches above the body, move up over the chest, down the arm, and off the fingertips. Discard the energy as before. Repeat two times. Then go from the waist, down the leg, and off the foot. Throw away energy, and repeat the entire movement twice more. (Fig. 9)

Move around to a waist position on the opposite side of the body and do the same thing over the left half of the body.

Immediately wash your hands in cold water. Dry your hands and return to the chest area on the right side of the body.

2) *Putting the Poles Back*

This corrects the energy flow (or strengthens an already correct flow) and is the key to everything in polarity. Failure to correct the flow can further overload the short circuits and further stress the body, which can result in *intensified* symptoms. Avoid this. Put the poles back first, so that all of the energy you share can easily flow properly.

FIGURE 10

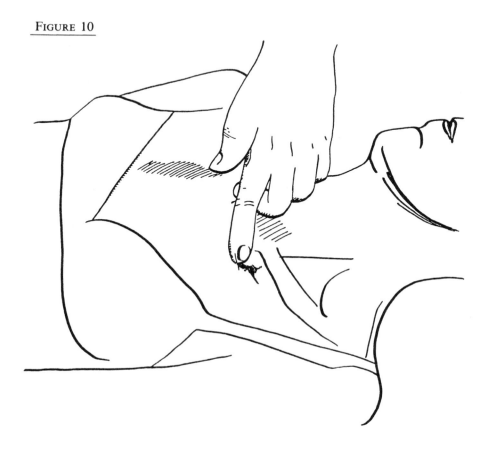

Place the left thumb and forefinger on acupuncture points Kidney-27. These are located in the indentation just below the clavicle (collarbone) and just outside the breastbone. (Fig. 10) Place your right hand on your partner's abdomen. Place the ball of the thumb over the navel, letting the thumb lie relaxed beside your fingers. Lightly agitate your left thumb and forefinger for fifteen to twenty seconds. Stop, and maintain this position for ten to fifteen seconds more.

The body is now back in normal polarity, and ready to receive further energy. You may now proceed to do any combination of holds on the front or back of the body.

Another method of putting the poles back, which can also be used on yourself, is to place the fingers and thumbs of both hands over the thymus, keeping the left hand slightly higher. Tap the thymus several times. (The thymus is located behind the top of the breastbone.)

3) *Stretching the Digits*

Every joint contains a mini-chakra which can become contracted, constricting the energy flow along the body. The hands and feet have numerous joints and therefore represent large energy transmitters with much potential for contraction. By stretching the fingers and the toes, we gently elongate the body and also stimulate all twelve primary acupuncture meridians, which results in a more balanced energy flow throughout the body.

I go around the body in a counterclockwise fashion, beginning with the right hand and then moving to the right foot, the left foot, and finishing with the left hand.

BE CAREFUL IN DOING ALL THE DIGIT WORK. DO NOT USE THIS ON PEOPLE WITH ARTHRITIS OR OTHER JOINT PROBLEMS. If it causes anyone pain, stop! People sometimes have very fragile skeletal systems or very sensitive nerves. It is wise to do all things gently, and stop at any sign of discomfort.

Working the digits is fairly easy. Hold your partner's right hand loosely in your left hand. Grasp the right thumb between your right thumb and forefinger and gently rotate your partner's thumb three times to the right (clockwise) and then three times to the left. Most people have enough flexibiliity to allow a circle two inches in diameter.

Then use your thumb and forefinger to move down the entire length of the thumb, in a mild zigzag fashion, first along the sides, and then along the top and bottom.

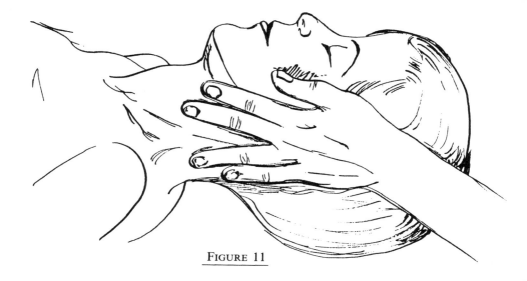

<u>FIGURE 11</u>

Next, grasp the thumb between your right forefinger and mid-dlefinger and slide off the thumb, pulling gently on the last one-and-a-half inches as you slide off. Your fingers will make a small snapping sound as they slap into each other. This motion stretches the thumb.

After you finish the thumb, use the same procedure with each of the four fingers, beginning with the forefinger. Once you are done with the hand, place it back on the table and move down to the right foot.

The work on the toes is essentially the same. However, go slowly: most toes are much less limber than fingers. Be careful with the large toe, which looks sturdy but which is actually quite easy to dislocate.

4) *Cradle*

This is a very powerful hold which can relieve nervousness and headaches. Sit or kneel at the top of the table so that you can comfortably place one hand on each side of your partner's neck. The right hand is on the right side, and the left hand is on the left side. Your thumbs go over your partner's ears. The forefingers go under the jaw and rest lightly on the carotid arteries, where the fingers can feel the pulse of the blood rushing to the head. The remaining fingers go straight down the neck. (Fig. 11)

This hold can accomplish several objectives. Pulses can be felt in many locations on the body, and they are rarely balanced (same rate of flow, same "beat" on each side of the body) when a session begins. But as the energy in the body becomes balanced, so do the pulses, so that they beat in unison on both sides of the body. Sometimes, at the beginning of a session, there may not be any evidence of pulses at all, but with a little effort, they will manifest for you.

It may take five minutes before you feel the barest pulse, but if you persist, you will eventually feel the pulse on each side of the neck. Then direct the pulses to beat at the same time, equally. Before long, they will. Picture the energy flowing evenly, up and down the body. Visualize the energy of the Universe flowing to you and going from your hands into the other person's body. Once you have the pulses beating strongly, in unison, congratulate yourself. Now that you have balanced the pulses in this hold, you will find that the flow of energy in subsequent holds will quickly reach optimum.

5) *Heel Cradle*

It is also possible to feel and balance the pulses (again from the heart) at the feet. Stand or sit at the foot end of the table. You can feel the pulse readily at a location approximately one-and-one-half inches above and behind the ankle, on the inside of the leg. It is easiest to feel the pulse with the forefinger of the left hand and the middlefinger of the right hand. Visualize the energy flowing through you: it will go wherever it is needed, and when enough has been absorbed, the body will become balanced, and so will the

FIGURE 12

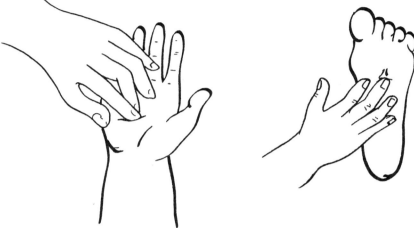

pulses. If you have succeeded with the cradle pulses, the heel pulses should balance within three minutes.

6) *Long Current*

It is generally felt that the longer the current, the stronger the current. The longest flow in the body is considered to be from one foot to its opposite hand (left foot to right hand, and right foot to left hand).

Stand on the right side of the body, waist high. Place the right middlefinger in the solar plexus area of the left foot. Then place the left forefinger in the solar plexus area of the right hand. (Fig. 12) Hold both points until you can feel a pulse at each location. Then move the right middlefinger to the same area on the right foot and the left forefinger to the same area in the the left hand and again hold until both pulses are felt.

7) *Shorter Currents*

These naturally constitute all currents except the longest flows. While much can be said for the long, strong flow, I believe in giving equal time to other currents. Shorter, concentrated currents can often break up congestion quickly, so if someone has problems in a particular area, I begin with very short currents and gradually lengthen them after the energy has begun to move freely.

8) *Hip to Opposite Shoulder*

This hold creates a stronger energy flow. Stand at the chest area along the right side of your partner's body. Place your right middlefinger over the left side of the pelvic bone, and your left forefinger over the right shoulder. When the pulse becomes strong, move your right middlefinger to the left side of the pelvic bone, and your left forefinger over the left shoulder. (Fig. 13) Many people find this hold comforting and relaxing.

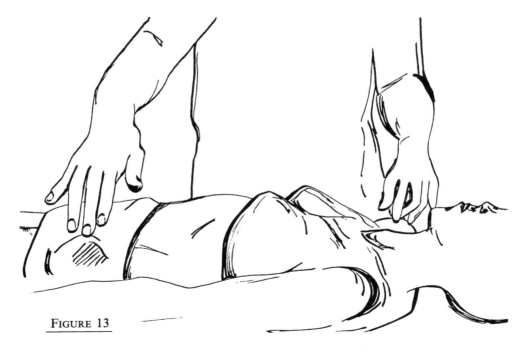

Figure 13

9) *Hip to Opposite Hand*

Place the right middlefinger over the left side of the pelvic bone, and the left forefinger on the solar plexus area of the right hand. After the pulses become strong, move your right middlefinger to the right side of the pelvic bone, and your left forefinger to the solar plexus area of the left hand. (Fig. 14)

[The next four holds for the front of the body can be done while seated or kneeling at the head of the table.]

10) *Temples*

Place your right middlefinger on your partner's right temple, and your left forefinger on your partner's left temple, and hold gently. This is wonderful for headaches, nervous tension, and eyestrain.

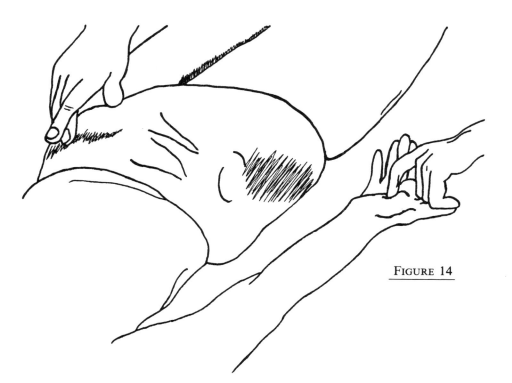

FIGURE 14

FIGURE 15

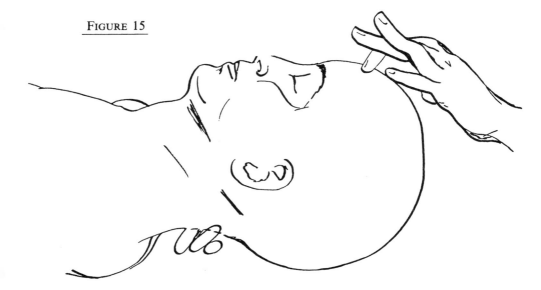

11) *Occiput to Top of Forehead (Frontal Eminence)*

This hold is used for overall rejuvenation or for headaches or nervous tension. Note that it incorporates two of the body's four switchboards, which automatically makes it powerful.

Place the right middlefinger in the hollow at the base of the skull (the area known as the occiput). Place the left forefinger in the middle of the hairline on the forehead. (Fig. 15) The pulses may become strong after fifteen seconds. People sometimes see colors during this hold.

12) *Occiput to Ajna*

This is similar. The right middlefinger stays on the occiput, but this time the left forefinger rests on the ajna center, between the eyebrows. (Fig. 16) This can be very calming. Quite a few people see colors here, too.

FIGURE 16

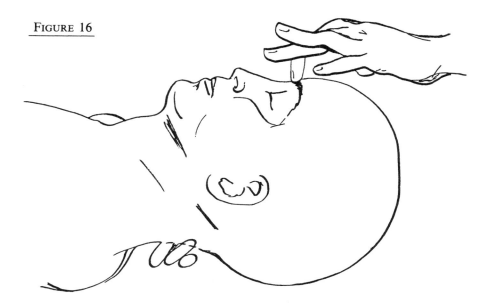

13) *Neck Points*

Everyone holds tensions in the neck and shoulder areas. Passing energy through the neck greatly relieves this congestion. Standing, sitting, or kneeling at your partner's head, place the left forefinger on the left side of the neck, and the right middlefinger on the right side of the neck, in parallel locations. The pulse usually comes quickly here. I generally send energy at locations one and three. If the person has neck complaints, throat problems, or excessive tension, I work all four locations until a strong pulse is established. (Fig. 17)

At this point, or whenever you have finished working on the front side of the body, repeat the 1) *Cleansing the Field* stroke.

If you are going to end the session here, immediately wash your hands. If you are going to work on the back of the body, have

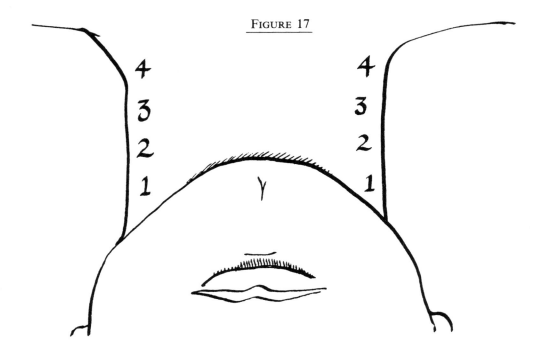

FIGURE 17

your partner turn over. Use the 1) *Cleansing the Field* stroke just as you did on the front of the body, pulling extraneous energy out of your partner's aura and flinging it away. *Immediately* wash your hands in cold water. Dry your hands and return to a waist position on the left side of your partner's body. Check your own breathing. Are you relaxed? Have your partner breathe deeply at least three times before you begin the work on the back of the body. If your partner seems self-conscious about the deep breathing, do it together, as before.

14) *Longest Flow*

This is done essentially the same way on the back as it is on the front of the body. Place the middlefinger of the right hand in the solar plexus area of the left foot, and then place the left forefinger in the solar plexus area of the right hand. Hold until you feel the

FIGURE 18

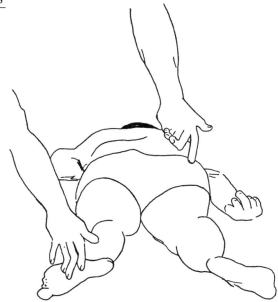

pulses in both spots. Then move your right middlefinger to the right foot and your left forefinger to the left hand. Hold again until both pulses are felt. You might want to spend a little extra time on this hold simply because it *is* giving the body a long and powerful flow. This will increase the depth of relaxaton for your partner.

15) *Foot to Opposite Hip*

Place your right middlefinger on the solar plexus area of the left foot and your left forefinger on the right hip, and hold until the pulsing becomes strong. (Fig. 18) Then move the right middlefinger to the right foot and the left forefinger to the left hip. Again hold for the pulse.

FIGURE 19

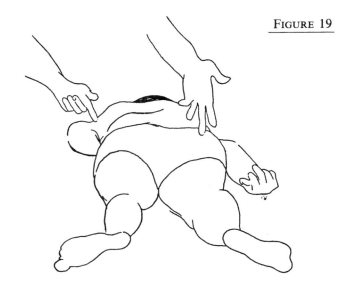

16) *Hip to Opposite Shoulder*

Place the left forefinger on the left shoulder and the right middlefinger on the right hip. (Fig. 19) Once the pulse has become strong and regular, move the left forefinger to the right shoulder and the right middlefinger to the left hip. Hold again until you feel a strong pulsing.

[CAUTION: DO NOT USE THE FOLLOWING TWO HOLDS ON PERSONS WITH VERY HIGH BLOOD PRESSURE OR THOSE WITH A TENDENCY TOWARD EPILEPSY.]

17) *Spinal Warmer*

Standing on your partner's left, place your right middlefinger on the coccyx (base of spine) and your left forefinger on the oc-

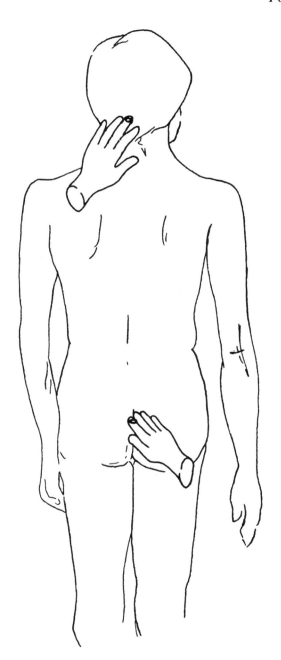

FIGURE 20

ciput (indentation at base of skull). (Fig. 20) This sends balancing energy the entire length of the spinal column. Please note that this hold incorporates two of the body's switchboards. It should, therefore, be considered a major hold, and should be used in every session, unless your partner has very high blood pressure or a tendency toward epilepsy.

Visualize a stream of energy flowing from your hands and through the spine. Many people report a noticeable increase in warmth in the spinal area during this hold.

18) *Chakra Balance*

This is a wonderful way to end a session. Chakras are vortices of energy located just in front of the spine. Pulses from the chakras may seem very subtle to you at first, but if you are patient and attentive, your attempts will be rewarded. Many people have blocks in the chakras. Such blockages are visible to clairvoyants, and result in discomfort in the physical areas nearest the chakras being blocked. Visualize the chakras coming back into balance with each other and with the flow of Universal energy streaming from your hands.

To begin, stand on your partner's left side. Place your right middlefinger on the coccyx and your left forefinger on the occiput. Your left hand will stay here for several parts of this hold. (Fig. 21) Once your fingers are in position, close your eyes and visualize clearly a strong flow of energy through yourself and into your partner. If, after two minutes, you have not felt the pulse in your right middlefinger, place the palm of your right hand over the chakra and massage gently but firmly for ten seconds. Hold the hand in that position until you feel the pulse. Then concentrate again on feeling the pulse simultaneously in both hands.

When the pulse has become strong and even, move to the next chakra. Place the right middlefinger on the spine in the small of the back near the waist, at the level of the 4th lumbar vertebra. Picture the flow of energy as before. If the chakra has not

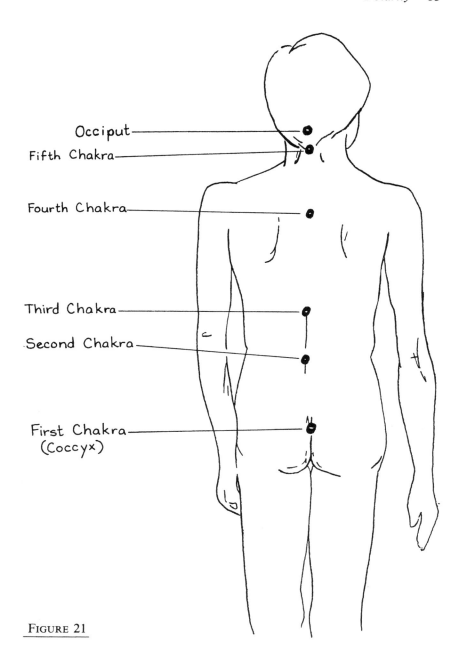

Occiput

Fifth Chakra

Fourth Chakra

Third Chakra

Second Chakra

First Chakra
(Coccyx)

FIGURE 21

responded after two minutes, use the palm-of-the-hand method described above.

The third chakra is on the spine near the bottom of the ribcage, at the level of the 8th thoracic vertebra. The left hand stays in position; the right middlefinger moves upward. Exhale, and be certain that you are relaxed.

The next chakra is on the spine between the shoulder blades, at the level of the 1st thoracic vertebra. The left hand remains where it is.

The fifth chakra is at the occiput, where your left forefinger has been all along. Now bring your right middlefinger up to join it. Feed both energies in, with the right finger just below the left one.

For the sixth chakra, your right middlefinger remains where it is, while the left forefinger finally gets to move around to the ajna center, between the eyebrows. Hold the left forefinger one-half inch away from this center. It is not necessary to touch it. Visualize the energy flowing between yourself and your partner. It may take a little longer to feel the pulse here, because you're not touching the skin, but relax and keep on. Some people will see colors here. (Fig. 22)

Once the pulse is established, congratulate yourself and move on to the final chakra. The right hand remains in position, and the left forefinger moves to the crown of the head. You may go as close as two inches; with practice, you will be able to feel the pulse at three or four inches from the surface of the body. (Fig. 23)

After the pulse has become strong and regular, slowly and gently withdraw your hands, beginning with the right hand.

Your partner will now be fully relaxed. In fact, your partner may have fallen asleep.

19) *Cleansing the Field*

Last, but never least, pull off the extraneous energy and fling it away as described earlier. Be certain that you wash your hands immediately.

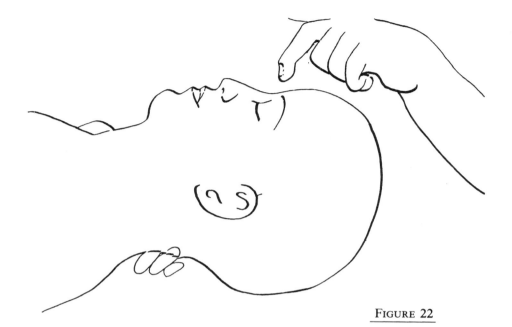

FIGURE 22

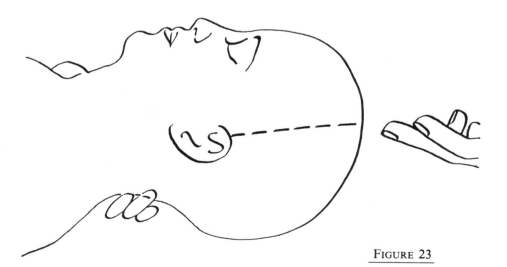

FIGURE 23

20) *Afterward*

If neither of you must hurry off, allow your partner to relax as long as s/he wants. Fifteen minutes of rest is very helpful. This lets the body utilize the energy it has absorbed for healing rather than for ordinary tasks, and this alone can multiply the effectiveness of the session. Many people also need a chance to readjust to "waking time," because they have experienced an altered state while relaxing with their eyes closed. My personal preference is for silence during the session, and then the playing of healing music in this resting interlude afterward, to enable the partner to gradually come back to waking consciousness, feeling extremely refreshed and rejuvenated.

Some people like to hug at the conclusion of a polarity session. But people differ in their ability to touch; some hug easily; some do not. And polarity affects people on many levels. You may find even your dearest friend or relative temporarily focused inward after a session. Try to let them choose the level of interaction that is comfortable for them. It is a good idea, anyway, to cultivate the ability to love as fully with your eyes as you can with your arms. A loving glance can convey more understanding than even the most robust or most passionate hug. I take my cue from the partner. If we have established a good rapport, and if the partner wishes to hug, I will. Otherwise, I simply smile. In either case, I send them a silent blessing.

10

ACUPRESSURE

Acupressure applies thumb pressure rather than needles to points on the acupuncture meridians in order to re-balance the flow of body energies. Stimulation of a point achieves the same results whether it is applied by needle, pressure, or electrical impulse. Such stimulation is known to: restore energy flow; increase blood supply; reduce pain; release wastes, which are then carried off by the lymph; stimulate endocrine function; and help restore both physical and mental relaxation.

ENERGY FLOW THROUGH THE MERIDIANS

Energy circulates through the twelve major meridians once every twenty-four hours, in the sequence shown on page 88.

These meridians occur bilaterally (one on each side of the body, left and right). The Governing Vessel (GV) and Conception Vessel (CV) run over the midlines of the body, front and back. They are often used in treatments, but are considered extra meridians. Some recently-discovered points are used, and are called "Extra" or "Special" points.

Diseases involving the twelve major meridians should be treated during the hours listed (p. 88), when the energy is flowing most strongly through the affected meridian and its related structures.

Sequence of Energy Circulation:

1. Lung (L)	3 AM –	5 AM
2. Large Intestine (LI)	5 AM –	7 AM
3. Stomach (St)	7 AM –	9 AM
4. Spleen (Sp)	9 AM –	11 AM
5. Heart (H)	11 AM –	1 PM
6. Small Intestine (SI)	1 PM –	3 PM
7. Bladder (Bl)	3 PM –	5 PM
8. Kidney (K)	5 PM –	7 PM
9. Pericardium (P)	7 PM –	9 PM
[Also known as Circulatory-Sex (C-S)]		
10. Triple Warmer (TW)	9 PM –	11 PM
11. Gall Bladder (GB)	11 PM –	1 AM
12. Liver (Liv)	1 AM –	3 AM

PAIN CONTROL

There are two types of nerves which transmit pain sensations, A-delta and C-fibers. A-delta nerves are comparatively thick and insulated; C-fibers are thinner and non-insulated. Impulses travel much faster in A-delta. (When we injure ourselves, we feel two kinds of pain: A-delta is immediate; C-fiber is more dull but longer lasting, and happens later than A-delta.) These nerves go to the spinal cord, where they contact cells connected with the brain. In this same region of the spinal cord (substantia gelatinosa) there are also large quantities of small nerve cells. Wall and Melzack proposed, in 1965, that these small cells served as a pain gate which could switch off or on the impulses coming from the pain nerves to the spinal cord.

Pain perception is partly controlled by signals from the brain and partly by A-beta fibers. These are mainly found in the skin and muscles; they are thick and insulated and end near the switching cells. A-beta fibers carry touch, pressure, and temperature sensations: when the sensations become too intense or too prolonged, the switches are turned off; when the sensations are too light, the switches are turned on. This helps us understand how deep pain can be ignored (following a major injury) and how miniscule pain at the skin level can seem very intense.

Rubbing or warming the skin will make the A-beta fibers switch off some of the pain. Some A-beta fibers end at principal acupuncture points; consequently, stimulation of these points will shut the pain gate. This concept is applied in using acupressure for anesthesia.

Recent research has discovered a number of different chemical messengers, or neuro-transmitters, which help convey information along nerve pathways. Some stimulate the brain, while others do not. One naturally-occurring family of substances which inhibit pain is known as *endorphins*. These chemicals block the further transmission of pain impulses. Professor Pomeranz in Toronto discovered that acupuncture used for twenty minutes to one hour liberated endorphins. So it is possible that many analgesic effects are really produced by stimulating the release of endorphins.

Endorphins have many roles beyond pain reduction. They appear to be a natural tranquilizer. They can cause joy and euphoria. The Chinese have known for thousands of years that acupuncture could be used for mood elevation. Ten to thirty minutes after stimulation begins, these effects may be noted. Pain transmissions are apparently blocked during happy periods. Happy people may be creating their own constant and natural high.

The pituitary is a primary source of endorphins; when the pituitary of cats is removed, acupuncture fails to affect the transmission of pain signals.

If you have severe or prolonged pain, it would certainly be worth trying acupressure for relief. While this would not solve your problem, it might suppress your pain while you work at removing the underlying cause. It is certainly preferable to treat pain via the body's own mechanisms than it is to introduce outside pain-killers. Prescription pain remedies rarely solve the problem, anyway, because they don't touch the cause, either. And dosages for high-powered drugs must often be increased as the body becomes tolerant to them, and of course, there is always the potential for addiction.

There are, however, an unfortunate thirty per cent of chronic pain patients who do not respond to acupuncture or morphine. Pomeranz believes that these people lack opiate receptors in the brain.

ACUPRESSURE TECHNIQUE

You can apply acupressure to yourself or to others, using your thumb. You can use the ball of your thumb, or, by placing the thumb at an angle, you can use the corner of the thumb. (Fig. 24) Press down, and vibrate the thumb slightly, while rotating it clockwise. Your index or middle finger may be substituted for the thumb.

Some people use light pressure, starting outside the point and making concentric circles inward, to stimulate or tonify related structures; and deep pressure, beginning at the point and moving outward in concentric circles, in order to sedate overactive points. Other practitioners make no such distinction and utilize the same pressure on all points. However, here as elsewhere, be alert and sensitive to any pain which may be noted during the treatment. Your pressure should create a ''good hurt'' on the point, not a deep or lasting pain. I recommend that you practice on yourself until you learn to recognize the difference.

People vary in their sensitivity to pain, so always ask people to report anything beyond mild discomfort. Points on the face and

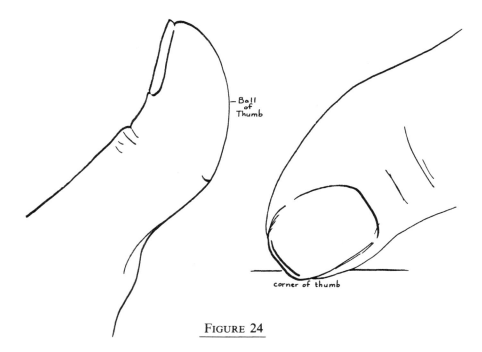

Ball of Thumb

corner of thumb

FIGURE 24

on the extremities are always more sensitive than those in other locations, so treat them accordingly. I prefer to begin light; if the person tolerates this well, I will then apply slightly deeper pressure.

The length of treatment can vary anywhere from a few seconds to several minutes. After consulting several sources, I generally pick between five and ten points and stimulate each point from five to seven seconds for the first session (treating the points on each side of the body). This gives the body a chance to begin correcting itself. If improvement is noted after the first session, then I treat the same points somewhat longer in subsequent sessions.

Use the body as your guide. It will tell you if you are overloading its pain thresholds. Some points may become sore after the treatment; this indicates that the chosen treatment was right and that the body is working to correct the malfunction. Once you gain confidence in acupressure's ability to help the body heal itself, you will probably opt for short and sweet treatments in most cases. Many people can learn to give themselves treatments, and this should be encouraged. Always help people become more responsible for their own well-being.

ACUPRESSURE POINTS

[CAUTION: (1) ACUPRESSURE IS NO SUBSTITUTE FOR PROMPT AND THOROUGH MEDICAL DIAGNOSIS AND TREATMENT OF ANY CONDITION. (2) NEVER PRESS ON AREAS AT OR NEAR THE SITE OF INJURY. IF IN DOUBT, DON'T!]

Many authors outline treatments for specific problems. My favorite authors to consult are Cerney, Chaitow, Chan, Dalet, and Tappan (see *References* for titles). I have used many of their suggested points, with good results. You can use one or more points for each condition; different authors give anywhere from one to fifteen points.

The following illustrations show the points which are most often recommended for the treatment of various problems.

[AGAIN, NEVER DIAGNOSE YOURSELF. SEEK PROMPT MEDICAL ADVICE FOR ANY CONDITION.]

1. Bl-60
   Outside of foot,
   behind ankle

   For: Ankle pain;
         Leg pain;
         Sciatica.

   FIGURE 25

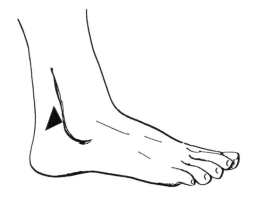

2. GB-20
   On head, behind
   and below ear

   For: Neck, head relief;
         Stiff neck.

   FIGURE 26

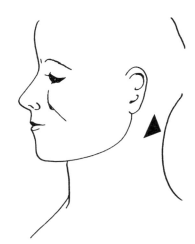

3. GB-21
   On shoulder
   For: Shoulder, neck,
        back pain.

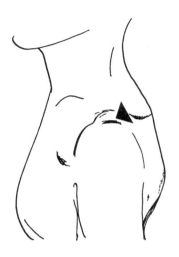

FIGURE 27

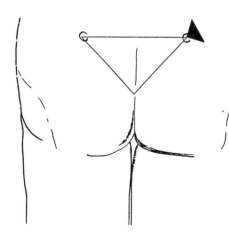

4. GB-30
   Near sacrum
   For: Hip, leg, low back
        pain; Sciatica.

FIGURE 28

5. GB-34
   Outside of leg,
   just below knee

   For: Indigestion; Dizziness;
        Knee pain.

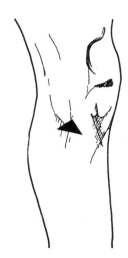

FIGURE 29

6. GB-36
   Outside of leg

   For: Tired legs.

FIGURE 30

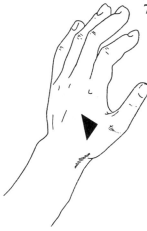

7. LI-4
   Outside of hand,
   just above joint
   of thumb and
   forefinger

For:
Analgesic; Headaches; Sore throat;
Toothache; Ankle pain; Common cold;
Insomnia; Nasal congestion; Fever; Eye
disease; Physical or mental exhaustion.

FIGURE 31

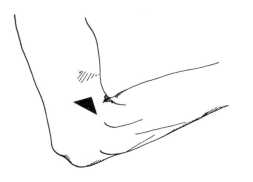

8. LI-11
   Outside of arm,
   just above elbow

   For: Shoulder, arm,
         elbow pain; Fever;
         Common cold.

FIGURE 32

9. LI-15
   Upper arm, front
   of shoulder
   For: Shoulder, arm,
      elbow pain.

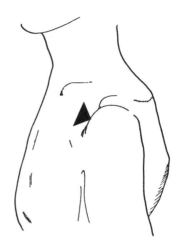

FIGURE 33

10. LI-20
    On face, outside of
    nostrils
    For: Sinus; Blocked nose.

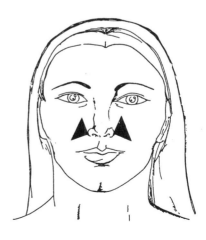

FIGURE 34

11. Liv-3
    Top of foot

    For: Headache; Dizziness;
         Lower back pain; Edema
         (Water retention).

    FIGURE 35

12. L-7
    Inside of wrist,
    about 1½'' above crease

    For: Headache; Neck
         pain; Cough; Facial pain.

    FIGURE 36

13. P-6

Inside of wrist,
middle, about 1''
above crease

For: Hiccups; Angina;
    Vomiting; Insomnia;
    Chest, stomach pain;
    Lost voice.

FIGURE 37

14. SI-3

Outside of hand,
just above base
of large knuckle

For: Neck pain; Deafness;
    Low back pain; Headache.

FIGURE 38

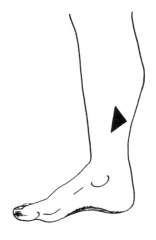

15. Sp-6
    Inside of leg,
    behind tibia

    For: Insomnia; Sexual
         dysfunctions; Menstrual
         problems; Urinary and
         bowel problems; Difficult
         labor; Motion sickness.

    FIGURE 39

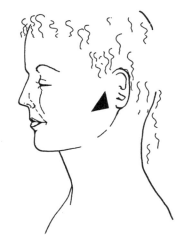

16. St-7
    In front of ear,
    in front of lower
    jaw

    For: Toothache.

    FIGURE 40

17. St-36

Front of leg,
about 3'' below
knee joint

For: General weakness;
Intestinal disturbances
and diseases; Hip and
leg ache; Anemia;
Headache' Abdominal pain;
Motion sickness; Impotence;
Diarrhea.

FIGURE 41

18. SP-1

(Special Point 1)
Between eyebrows

For: Headache; Dizziness;
Nose; Sinus.

FIGURE 42

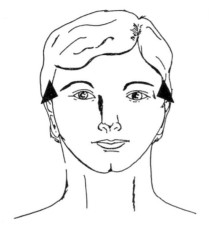

19. SP-2
    (Special Point 2)
    On temple, about
    1'' from end of eye

    For: Migraine; Eye diseases;
         Toothache; Insomnia.

FIGURE 43

20. CV-12
    Midway between tip
    of breastbone
    and navel

    For: Vomiting; Motion
         sickness; Indigestion;
         Abdominal pain.

FIGURE 44

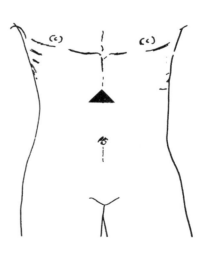

21. CV-22
   In indentation at
   top of breastbone

   For: Asthma; Cold with
   cough; Lung congestion.

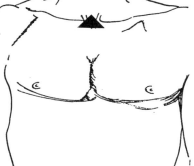

FIGURE 45

22. H-7
   Outside edge, in
   crease, at palm

   For: Insomnia;
   Nervousness;
   Palpitation.

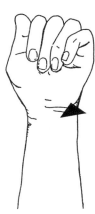

FIGURE 46

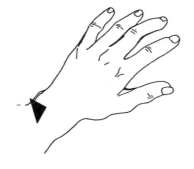

23. TW-5
    About 2'' up from
    wrist crease,
    back of hand

    For: Prevent colds;
         Hand, wrist ache.

    FIGURE 47

24. P-7
    On wrist crease,
    palm side of hand

    For: Sunburn; First
         degree burns.

    FIGURE 48

25. GV-26

    About 1/3 of way
    between base of
    nose and upper lip,
    on midline of body

    For: Shock; Fainting.

    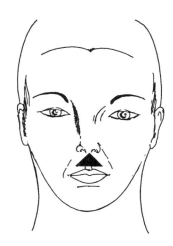

    FIGURE 49

26. K-25

    4 finger-widths
    above right nipple,
    in space between
    ribs 2 & 3

    For: Pain from
         injury; Mental or
         physical shock.

    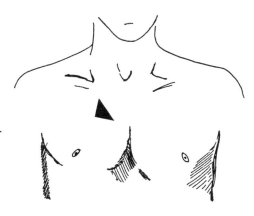

    FIGURE 50

EXERCISE TO BALANCE AND ENERGIZE

The following drawings (Fig. 51) show the points where the meridians begin or end. By massaging the toes and fingers, you can quickly stimulate the twelve traditional meridians. Try to cultivate the habit of massaging these areas at least once a day—perhaps first thing in the morning, or just before dinner. If circumstances permit, try treating yourself to this energy-enhancer during your work breaks.

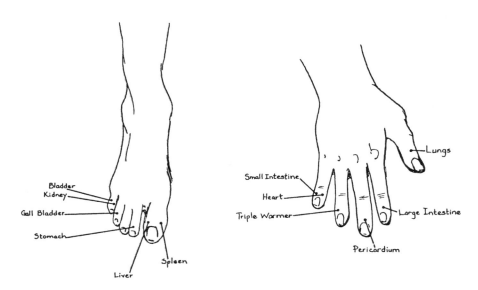

FIGURE 51

11

REFLEXOLOGY

Reflexology is a method of treating the entire body through the feet and the lower legs. The Chinese believe that the whole body is mirrored in the eye, ear, palm of the hand, and bottom of the foot. They have used finger pressure on the feet (needles were too painful here) for 5,000 years to bring physiological functions back to normal.

Then, in the 1800's, Head discovered viscero-cutaneous (internal organ to skin) and cutaneo-visceral reflex effects in the body. We now know that all parts of the body are intimately interrelated. Research has proven that the complete body can be found in miniature in the feet, hands, eyes, and ears. Acupuncturists can treat the whole body, using only ear points.

In the early part of this century, Dr. William H. Fitzgerald discovered that *direct* pressure on certain areas of the body produced analgesic or anesthetic effects in a corresponding part of the body. This led Fitzgerald to divide the body into zones. (Fig. 52) (Some people believe that Fitzgerald merely "rediscovered" Chinese foot massage and brought it to the attention of U.S. doctors in 1913 as "Zone Therapy.") Edwin Bowers began working with Fitzgerald. Dr. George Starr White and Joseph Selbey Riley, M.D., were other early proponents.

In the early 1930's, a therapy assistant of Dr. Riley's named Eunice Ingham discovered that the feet contained a map of the

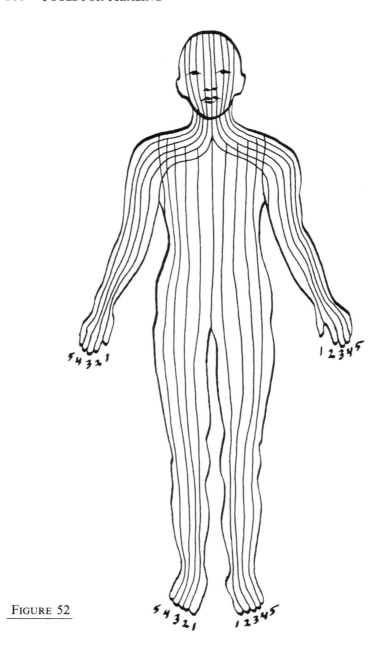

FIGURE 52

body, and that *alternating* pressure produced other therapeutic effects—not just the elimination of pain. Ingham is considered the founder of foot reflexology.

Ingham recommended that treatments be given no oftener than twice a week, to allow the body to gently and easily return to a state of normalcy or homeostasis. In working with chiropractors and osteopaths, she also discovered that working the spinal reflexes in the feet—prior to other corrective measures—gave additional relaxation and made the effect of the practitioner's adjustment last longer. Ingham also recognized that the mind and the emotions could greatly affect the physical body and cautioned that one should work toward balance and understanding in all areas of life.

Reflexology is gaining in popularity partly, perhaps, because of its simplicity, and partly because almost everyone likes to have the feet massaged. Even people who are usually reluctant to have their bodies touched find that they enjoy a reflexology treatment.

Like polarity, reflexology is not so much a method of diagnosis as it is a means for discovering where blockages in the body's energy flows are occurring. "Treatment" then becomes simple: you aid the body by working the entire foot to release all blockages so that the energy can once again flow freely. Responses to treatment are individual. One treatment can bring remarkable relaxation; it cannot, however, bring instant health. It sometimes takes a while to uncover the true cause of any chronic symptoms, so relief may be immediate or gradual.

Working the feet causes corresponding areas of the body to relax. This relaxation allows the free flow of both energy and nutrients to all body cells and organs. Stress has opposite effects: stress causes the body to become tense, which restricts the flow of nutrients and inhibits the proper functioning of all organs and systems. Reflexology can therefore be very usefully employed as an anti-stress therapy. It is easy to learn; friends, neighbors, or relatives can trade treatments. Reflexology is also beneficial for children. Trading reflexology treatments often brings people closer together.

For serious or chronic problems, though, you may want to consult an experienced professional reflexologist. Look in the Yellow Pages under Massage. Chiropractors or natural food stores may also be able to refer you to local reflexologists. Because the hands and feet are so readily accessible, reflexology is also ideal as a means of self-treatment.

REMEMBER, REFLEXOGY IS NO SUBSTITUTE FOR MEDICAL DIAGNOSIS AND TREATMENT. PLEASE DO NOT ATTEMPT TO DIAGNOSE YOURSELF. GET SEVERAL MEDICAL OPINIONS, AND THEN FEEL FREE TO USE REFLEXOLOGY IN ADDITION TO MEDICAL TREATMENTS.

Reflexology will always be beneficial, even if it does nothing more than counteract your stress. It would be unrealistic, however, to ask reflexology alone to cure a fast-growing cancer. By combining the best possible treatments, you maximize your body's ability to heal itself completely, and as quickly as it can.

TECHNIQUE

You can use the ball of the thumb, the corner of the thumb, or in smaller areas, the tips of your fingers.

Various methods of moving the thumb and establishing contact on the foot have been described. Here, as in all other healing techniques, practice will teach you which method is most effective and efficient for you.

The amount of pressure varies and is greatly dependent upon the person you are working on. A person in good condition and with a high tolerance for pain will be able to withstand about ten pounds of pressure. (You can use your bathroom scale to practice varying amounts of pressure from zero to ten.) Others who are more tender, or who have tender areas, may only be able to tolerate a pressure equivalent to two pounds. *Always* alter your treatment to fit the client or partner. Go slowly at the beginning and gradually work up to the person's tolerance level.

Method 1:   Bend your right thumb, and place it on the back of your left hand. Push your thumb slightly forward, while at the same time straightening it. Then pull the thumb back a bit while bending it. Repeat these two movements. Once you get the hang of it, start practicing a creeping motion up your left arm. It is a good idea to practice on your own hand or foot. The more you practice, the more natural and comfortable all your techiques will become.

Method 2:   Bend the first joint of the right thumb. Use your left hand to hold the thumb below its first joint. Practice bending the first joint while the rest of the thumb remains stationary. Then put the outside corner of your right thumb on one of your legs. As you bend the thumb, let it rock a little; this allows it to "walk" forward slightly.

It is important to practice with both hands so that eventually you can develop the same strength and finesse within each.

BASIC CONSIDERATIONS

1. Blockage of energy is registered as sensitivity, soreness, or pain. This tells you that something is happening in a particular zone or even across several zones. According to zone therapy, direct pressure applied anywhere within a zone will affect the entire zone.

2. In reflexology, all zones are treated via their representative areas on the feet. There is one notable exception to this: the right half of the brain controls the left side of the body, and the left half

of the brain controls the right side of the body; therefore, when the brain (or central nervous system) is involved, treat the *opposite* foot.

3. If the person has corns or callouses, s/he should be obtaining podiatric treatments. Ingrown nails, thickened nails, bunions, and displaced bones also affect the foot and any zones connected with them. Encourage people to seek professional care whenever it is warranted. *Avoid working on painful areas such as cuts, bruises, or blisters.*

4. A short treatment can be given in twenty minutes, once you get the knack of reflexology. Thirty to forty-five minutes is normal for a session.

5. If the person is ill, give shorter treatments. Results are usually evident in four to eight weeks, although this varies from person to person, and severe or chronic problems may be slower in showing any progress. Treatments are preferably given twice a week at first.

6. Clients or partners should be encouraged to work on themselves (self-treatment) between treatments. As the person's feet return to normal (no pain during treatment), the frequency of sessions can be reduced.

7. Working the kidney area of each foot thoroughly will help to minimize any reactions caused by the release of waste products into the person's system. Even the sturdiest-looking people can have intense reactions to treatment. This is another good reason to undertreat, especially for the first few sessions.

8. Your environment can also enhance the healing process. You may want to play soft, quiet, relaxing music. Or your partner may prefer silence. Everyone has unique requirements for relaxation.

9. Your partner may have questions about reflexology, nutrition, healing, or disease. There are several ideas to keep in mind here.

First, make it clear that you are not a medical doctor and so cannot diagnose, prescribe, nor treat specific problems. You are trying *to help the body return to a state of normalcy so that it can heal itself.* The whole body works together.

Second, be careful of everything you say. There are usually two levels to a question—one literal, and one not. Use your intuition to determine the real question. (If people start telling you their family medical history, it may really be because they think heredity is everything, whereas each of us can do a great deal to make the best of any genetic predisposition.) Ask leading questions to see what the person knows. Encourage everyone to do his/her own research. Remember that a positive attitude is always an asset.

Third, meet the partner at his or her level of understanding. Encourage the person to learn more, but begin slowly. Someone who has never read a book on nutrition is not going to be able to follow an intricate explanation on why some bodies have difficulty absorbing calcium. On the other hand, give people credit for a high level of intelligence. Most people have it, whether or not they are using it actively. Also, do not pretend that you know what is best for your partner, in the present or in the future. What everyone needs most is loving acceptance. Make that your gift to every partner. People often move into a period of growth when they feel accepted.

10. *Contraindications.*   Thrombophlebitis: if there is redness, swelling, pain, and greater warmth in the heart area of the left foot, *do not treat the foot.* Treat the left hand instead.

Lightheadedness or free perspiration during the treatment means that the body is attempting to get rid of toxins too fast. If this happens, simply treat the pituitary gland.

DESSERTS

Desserts are massage movements which can be used before, during, and after reflexology in order to help the partner relax and enjoy the session. These become even more important if your partner has a great degree of soreness, because desserts enable you to provide quiet moments in between the painful ones.

1. Hold the heel of the foot in one hand, and, using the other hand, turn the foot first clockwise three times, and then counterclockwise three times.

2. Hold the heel in one hand, use the second hand to push the toes toward the body (upward) and then away from the body (downward).

3. Place your left fist against your partner's foot. Gently pull the toes downward with your right hand as you push against the sole with your left fist.

4. Cup the ankle in the palms of your hands and roll the ankle from side to side between your palms.

5. Cup the heel in the palms and roll from side to side.

6. Place the hands on either side of the foot and roll the sides of the foot gently, rapidly alternating your hands. (Fig. 53)

7. Tap the sole of the foot with your fingers.

REFLEXOLOGY TREATMENT

Before beginning, wash your hands. Have your partner resting comfortably, with the spine straight. Your partner should be sit-

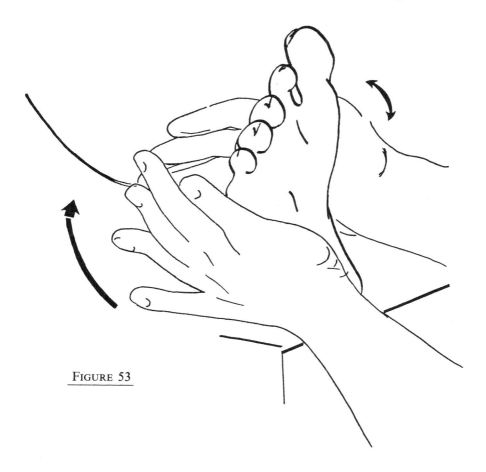

FIGURE 53

ting, reclining, or lying comfortably, with the feet elevated, and shoes and hosiery removed. You should be seated in front of the person's feet. Always have your fingernails short.

Ask about cuts or bruises or blisters, and avoid irritating any such area. Invite your partner to take several deep breaths. You may wish to do some deep breathing yourself, to assist the relaxation process. This is also a good time to visualize yourself as a grounded and receptive channel for healing energies. You may

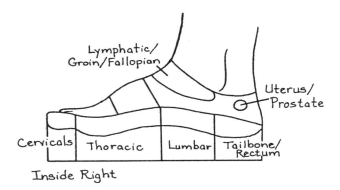

Inside Right

FIGURE 54A

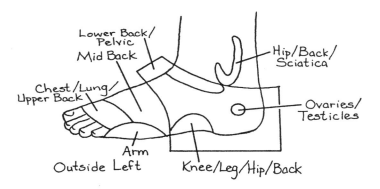

Outside Left

also picture a protective shield around yourself which prevents you from absorbing negative energies. It is important for you to remain comfortable throughout the session, because your level of relaxation is transferred automatically to your partner. And, as always, the more relaxed you are, the more healing energy you can convey.

Just below the ball of the foot, and toward the center, is the solar plexus reflex point (see illustrations of entire foot and lower leg areas, in Fig. 54A and 54B). Apply medium pressure here, on

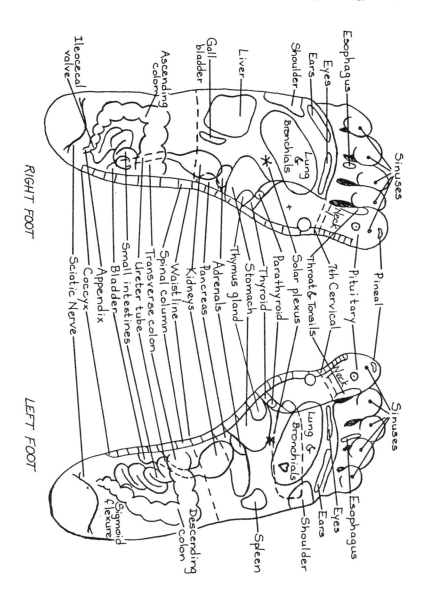

FIGURE 54B

both feet at the same time, for about one minute. Start with light pressure and gradually deepen it. Many people will have soreness here, so be gentle. Have your partner take several deep breaths. Holding the solar plexus reflex helps the entire body to relax. Visualize the energy going through your thumbs and into the feet, helping your partner to relax.

Then begin with the right foot. You may find it easier to use the right hand on the left foot and the left hand on the right foot; some people use this system, while others use both hands interchangeably.

Start with the big toe, also known as the great toe. Move it in a circular motion. Hold it with your thumb and first two fingers, and move it in a circular motion, three times clockwise, and then three times counterclockwise.

Then hold the toe, on the sides, between your thumb and forefinger, and using a sort of rocking motion, gently inch your thumb and forefinger up the sides of the toe. This stretches the toe slightly and helps free any blockages within the toe itself.

Apply these same techinques to the four smaller toes.

Then return to the large toe. Press on the pituitary center (in the middle of the ball of the great toe). Most people have some tenderness at this point, because the pituitary is the master gland and tends to be overworked in almost everyone.

Another point which is almost always tender is found on the inside of the big toe. It reflexes to the outside base of the neck —where many of us hold considerable tension. Be gentle here.

Work the entire area on the large toe: front, sides, and back. The large toe relates to the head and neck; consequently, this is a very important area.

Next, go halfway down the side of the big toe on the inside of the foot. The reflexes to the cervical vertebrae begin here, and those for the rest of the spine follow down along the inner edge of the foot. It is most important to cover this area thoroughly, because the spinal nerves contribute greatly to the correct functioning of the body. Many people have soreness along the spine, and thus you should probe gently at first and then go more deeply. Because the spine affects the entire body, your partner may noticeably relax after you work these reflexes.

Now that you have worked the inside edge of the foot, go to the outer edge and work it from the base of the small toe to the heel. This helps the flow of the lymphatic system.

Next, return to the four smaller toes, and work each one completely (front and back and both sides) as you did the large toe. Each of the smaller toes has reflexes to the sinuses.

Your hand positions, in working the area beneath the toes, on the bottom of the foot, become a little more elaborate. Use your left hand to move the toes backward slightly so that your right thumb has better access to the base of the toes and the small shelf between the toes and the foot. Probe the entire area from side to side at the base of the toes. You may work in either direction, but keep your thumb going forward at all times.

It is important to remember that even though many people have drawn many representations of how they think the body is reflected in the foot, our main concern is to relax the entire foot and thereby relax the entire body. Soreness at any point simply tells us that a blockage exists and that the energy flow there needs to be restored. There is no necessity to know, or to determine, that any particular segment of the body is involved. The body often stores pain or discomfort far from its source, so diagnosis based upon the site of pain can be misleading or wrong. In short, you don't need diagnosis. Concentrate instead on what counts: restoring the energy flow. Let the soreness show you where to direct the energy; that is its only legitimate purpose. Keep returning to areas of soreness until all the pain disappears.

Throughout the treatment, anywhere that you encounter soreness, you can have your partner "breathe through" the sore spot. Have your partner visualize the breath coming in through the spot, and then have the partner exhale loudly, with a sigh, through the same spot. This technique often brings a remarkable reduction of soreness within two to four breaths.

Once you have finished the area at the base of the toes, you can proceed to cover the rest of the bottom of the foot, using your thumbs. There is a method you can use to cushion your partner's foot and give yourself greater leverage. If you are going to use your right thumb, wrap your left hand around your partner's left foot, placing your fingers on the top of the foot. Then, once your left hand is in position, place the fingers of your right hand over the left-hand fingers. This leaves your right thumb free to work at the correct angle, and you can adjust the leverage between your two hands. An added benefit is that energy from your left hand will constantly be flowing into your partner's foot, so that you are sending energy into the foot from top and bottom (left hand and right thumb). This helps relax the entire zone, front to back and top to bottom.

Each foot is worked twice. Initially, cover the entire foot carefully to uncover any blockages. This helps relax and heal the entire body. Most reflexologists treat the right foot first, and then the left. After you have completely worked the foot, go back and re-work all the sore or painful areas that you noted the first time through. Then work the second foot. After you have fully worked both feet, you can alternate back and forth from foot to foot to cover any remaining sore spots. Or, have your partner concentrate on removing stubborn blocks through the breathing technique outlined above.

As you are moving over the feet, you will want to alter your techniques and positions. This will help you follow the contours of the foot in order to give a thorough treatment. It will also enable you to alternately rest your thumbs and fingers. Practice and patience will build up the strength in your hands, wrists, and forearms.

Many people start at the toes and work their way toward the heel, working across the foot at each level. Others start with the toes and then work the foot from toe to heel, lengthwise. I know one therapist who combines the above methods, covering the foot first crosswise and then up-and-down before spending additional time on painful areas. You can devise any system you like, so long as you remember to cover the entire foot.

After completing the massage on the bottom of the first foot, turn your attention to the top of the foot. You may find that your fingers work better for some of the work here. Work the area around the heel, massaging gently on the inside and the outside. Quite a few people show tenderness here, so begin lightly. I often work the inside of the foot with one hand and the outside with the other. This again surrounds the foot with energy. Come forward from the heel toward the toes, working slowly.

Next work the area around the ankles, on both sides of the foot. Fingers are especially useful here. Then slip behind the ankles and work from the heel upward to an area about two inches higher than the ankle, along the back of the leg. This area may be very congested and tender.

The final area to work is found in front of the ankle, between the ankle and the toes. Work from the ankle toward the toes. Fingers fit very well in the grooves along the top of the foot. This section relates to the lymph glands, and you can help drain the lymph system by working the top and bottom of the foot simultaneously. To do this, put your forefinger on the top of the foot, and your thumb underneath. Work the areas between the tendons and the bones with a squeezing and massaging motion.

If you wish, you can return to any areas which showed soreness before. Concentrate on these areas as you quickly cover the foot a second time. Your partner will probably notice less soreness everywhere this time through. Nevertheless, be considerate of your partner's tolerance levels, and do not push for maximum pain tolerance until you and the partner have been working together

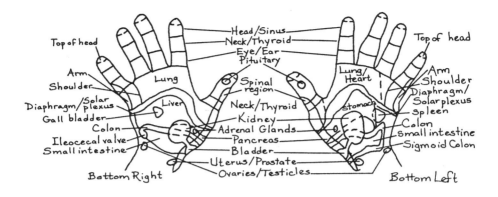

FIGURE 55

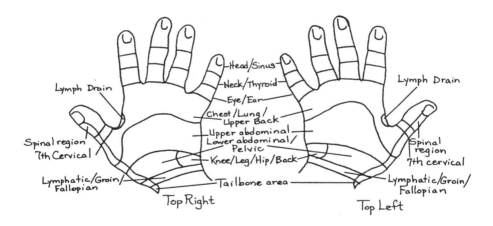

for some time. Even then, why should Superpain be any more useful than simple pain? It *is* possible to cause the body to release an overload of toxins, and this always results in great discomfort for your partner. So it is kinder of you, and wiser, to go slowly and let the body disperse toxins bit by bit.

Always be considerate of the other person. Do not try to prove how "good" you are by how much pain you can elicit from another person's body. Causing unnecessary pain is a sign of selfish, invasive touch. Don't do this to others, and, just as importantly, don't let others cause unnecessary pain when they are working on you, either.

If you haven't already been using the dessert techniques, now is the perfect time to add some in. Finish the foot by pulling off energy three times and flinging it away. Place your hands around the ankles and move off the foot slowly.

Then do the left foot, covering it as completely as you did the right.

Afterward, you may want to hold the solar plexus area on both feet again for a moment, to reinforce the total body relaxation. When you have finished, immediately wash your hands in cold water and dry them.

If time permits, it is beneficial for your partner to rest for a few minutes. Many people feel slightly sleepy following a treatment. I always do, for the first fifteen minutes afterward; then my body seems to swing into gear again, and I feel completely refreshed, and recharged with energy.

HANDS

Treatments on the hands may be given in the same general way. Hands, however, are considerably more tender than feet (most of the time), so alter your pressure accordingly. You will tend to find less soreness in the hands. This may be because we use the hands more. Some people feel that waste products settle more in the feet, due to gravity. Partners should be encouraged to do self-treatment on both hands and feet. (Fig. 55)

12

MASSAGE

In massage, we manipulate the soft tissues of the body for various purposes, including: pain relief, passive exercise, relaxation, and to increase the range of motion. Because it has such widespread applications, almost everyone can benefit from the correct use of massage. There are times, however, when massage is not indicated; and these are the times when it is particularly effective to use polarity. So let's establish a basic premise: *When in doubt, don't massage; use polarity!*

Massage, too, is thought to have originated in China. A century ago, an ancient Chinese text was translated into French, and this probably became the basis for the system of Swedish massage developed by Per Henrik Ling. French terminology still prevails in describing the five basic kinds of strokes: 1) *effleurage* (gliding); 2) *petrissage* (kneading); 3) *tapotement* (striking); 4) *friction* (compressing); and 5) *vibration* (shaking).

Massage is really the hardest hands-on therapy to learn, because it requires many things from the practitioner. You must feel comfortable with the human body; many people must develop the ability to touch others therapeutically. Second, you must educate your hands, arms, and back, because massage motions employ all three as a team. Third, you must have, or acquire, the ability to move your body gracefully and to shift your weight easily from one leg and foot to the other. Fourth, the hands must learn to communicate with your brain and mind, in order to interpret the condition of the body tissues they contact.

As in any other art, you begin with the basics and gradually work yourself up to higher and higher levels of understanding and achievement. The most basic thing you must have is the desire to help. Everything else can be learned, and, given sufficient practice, will become automatic. This enables you, in time, to interact intuitively with others during massage. And here, as in other forms of healing, the more levels you interact on, the greater the potential for both short- and long-term results.

BASIC RULES

1. Pressure is always applied on the stroke *toward the heart*. This aids the circulation of both blood and lymph.

2. Whenever possible, at least one hand should remain in contact with the partner during the entire treatment. This eliminates any guessing about where you are, and such continuous touch is very reassuring.

3. It is important to provide a quiet and relaxing environment. Unplug the telephone!

4. Every massage should begin with light pressure and gradually work up to the most comfortable degree of pressure for your partner. Once this level has been reached, you gradually work toward light strokes again to finish the massage.

5. Avoid the actual site of any injury, as well as the tissues surrounding it.

6. Know the partner's medical history, past and present.

7. Be alert, during massage, for any changes in your partner. A sudden tensing, moving, or jumping means that something is happening. Ask what your partner is experiencing.

8. Massage should only be done if the pulse rate and the body temperature are normal.

9. A short rest period should precede and follow every massage.

10. Avoid giving or receiving a massage for two hours after a meal.

11. Massages can be short or long. Even a five-minute massage by a skillful practitioner can accomplish many physiological and reflex effects. Local massages can be done for up to fifteen minutes. A complete body massage takes about an hour.

12. Always proceed cautiously, and go slowly, especially if you are working with strangers. Some people want human touch desperately. Most people consider themselves to be in excellent health whether they have been taking good care of themselves or not. Other people will try to fool themselves, and you, into thinking they are healthy when they know better. And some people will deny any prior knowledge of symptoms that you will spot immediately.

Your intuition will tell you when other people are being less than candid. You have two options, and you might choose to use them together. One, it is almost always safe to do a light backrub. Two, it is always safe to do polarity, for at least a short period of time.

13. Consider massage to be a dance in which you are constantly using your whole body. Always use your knees and body weight to move and to get any needed leverage. Once you learn how to use

your body in this way, you will be able to work almost indefinitely without getting tired. Practice moving your weight and shifting your body weight from one leg to the other. [See the chapter on *Exercise—Moving Your Body.*]

14. In all massage techniques, you want your hands to become as "liquid" as possible so that they can follow the contours of each part of the body. You must be able to feel and interpret the condition of the body structures as you move over them. Relaxation is vital here, because your hands must be relaxed in order for you to begin sensing anything about your partner through them.

15. Scientific massage treatments favorably influence almost every organ of the body. The key word here is *scientific.* You must understand how the body works, and when to use or not use certain methods, depending upon the age and condition of the person you are working on. Unrecognized and undiagnosed conditions can be made worse—as can recognized and diagnosed ones—by massage. You should know as much as possible about the physical health of someone before attempting any massage beyond a light backrub. Even gentle stimulation produces reflex effects locally or throughout the body. Direct pressure produces both reflex and mechanical effects.

16. *Contraindications: Do not give anything other than a light backrub when any of the following are present:* 1) hypertension (high blood pressure); 2) cancerous tumor; 3) diabetes; 4) kidney inflammation; 5) thrombosis, aneurism, or a heart condition; 6) acute inflammation (avoid these areas); 7) frostbite; 8) bone fractures (unhealed); 9) diseases of muscle, bone, or skin (beware of active infections under the skin); 10) recently torn muscles, tendons, ligaments (*do not massage any muscles which show any sign of injury, following athletic exertion, until after a physician has been consulted*); 11) osteoporosis (thinning of the bones; common

in elderly women, and some women at all ages); 12) arthritis (during inflamed stages); 13) appendicitis; 14) heavy menstrual flow; 15) following recent major surgery; 16) anorexia; 17) cancer; 18) obstructed bowel; 19) varicose veins; 20) abdomen, during pregnancy; 21) abdomen, when there are intestinal disorders; 22) fever.

Lubricants and Oils: Use and Removal

Various lubricants and oils may be used. Peanut oil, sesame oil, safflower oil, pure olive oil, and organic coconut oil are often preferred, but any lanolin-based cream may be used, and mineral oil or baby oil will also suffice. Always have a variety of oils on hand and consult your partner to find out if s/he is allergic to any oils. The best oils are cold-pressed, and they will remain fresh longer if capped tightly and kept refrigerated.

It is always better to use too little than too much lubricant, and some authorities even recommend that no lubricant be used. Experiment and see what works best for you. You want to be able to clearly feel the body under your hands, and yet you need to eliminate any friction so that your hands can move freely. Massage strokes are intended to be smooth, flowing, and rhythmical, so an ideal lubricant will allow freedom of movement over the body without making the body so slippery that your hands slide around without really feeling or affecting the body structures underneath.

All these lubricants can be removed with alcohol (for a stimulating effect) or with soap and warm water (for a relaxing effect) at the end of the session.

Massage Strokes

There are three basic categories of massage strokes, and each one is used to achieve certain effects.

1. Gliding (*effleurage*). This is often called "the long stroke," or "stroking." Gliding strokes are commonly used to apply lubricants at the start of massage, to make the transition between other massage strokes, and to end the massage.

Gliding includes any stroke that seems to simply move over the skin. The hands mold themselves to the parts of the body they encounter, and the stroking is done with firm, even pressure, toward the heart. Sensitive hands can locate immediately any tender or sore areas. In the beginning minutes of massage, always use light pressure; in the middle stages of massage, this type of stroking may be done more deeply.

Stroking movements are performed with the thumb, fingers, or palm of the hand. The whole hand is used on larger areas; thumbs, or even fingertips, are used to massage smaller areas. Thus the pressure can be altered to perform any range of depth from superficial to deep.

2. Compression (*friction*). There are three families of strokes in this category. Friction is created by the resistance between your hands and your partner's body.

Compression movements squeeze and rub the skin and also squeeze the underlying tissues. These motions help to prevent stiffness after exertion or exercise. Here again, it is important to begin gently and to slowly increase the pressure as you work gradually into the deeper tissues. Fleshy areas will tolerate more pressure than bony areas. Always be mindful of your partner's reaction.

Compression is done by making small circular motions with the fingertips, thumb, or even the heel of the hand. These motions penetrate the tissue by means of moving the tissue masses underneath the skin. Pressure should be increased and decreased gradually in order to get the maximum impact from this type of stroke.

a) Kneading (*petrissage*) is vigorous and is usually done on the abdomen, back, and extremities. Skin and muscles are lifted and then rolled, or squeezed, with firm pressure. Here you want to press or roll the muscles. This helps remove waste products from the tissues and also assists the blood flow back to the heart. Use minimal lubricant, in order to be able to pick up the skin and muscles.

b) Friction motions move along the surface of the skin, affecting the skin and underlying tissues without picking them up to squeeze them. They are, instead, gently moved away momentarily from their normal position.

c) Shaking (*vibration*). Here, the hand or fingers, placed against the body, move back and forth slightly and so rapidly that they vibrate the tissues underneath. An electrical vibrator may also be used, to provide more continuous movement. Prolonged vibration produces numbness.

This type of stroking soothes when done lightly (as with the limbs, to help them relax), and stimulates when applied deeply (as in the buttocks). Vibration is often applied after other strokes, because it helps the muscles remain loose and also enhances circulation to the area.

3. Striking (*tapotement*), also known as Percussion. In these methods, the hands strike the body. There is a wide range of striking methods: hacking, cupping, slapping, tapping, and pinching. Any series of rapid, brisk, alternating blows designed to induce stimulation in the tissues falls into this category. These techniques are considered particularly important for preparing an athlete for the start of his or her event.

CAUTION: THESE MOTIONS SHOULD ALWAYS BE USED WITH CARE. They stimulate the body and excite the metabolism, and some people can easily become overstimulated. NEVER USE THESE TECHNIQUES ON SENSITIVE AREAS OR WHERE MUSCLES ARE VERY CONTRACTED. MISUSE CAN CAUSE BRUISING AND INTERNAL INJURIES. NEVER USE THESE METHODS ON VERY FRAIL, VERY ILL PEOPLE, OR ON PREGNANT WOMEN, OR CHILDREN, OR ANIMALS.

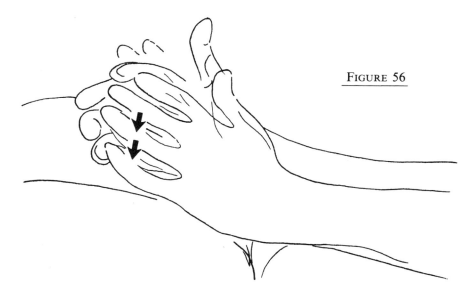

FIGURE 56

a) *Hacking* is done with the hands and wrists completely re-laxed, moving up and down alternately, with the hands sideways, and striking soft, brisk blows with only the tips of the last three fingers on each hand. (Fig. 56) Some people strike with the lower edge of the hand and the little finger. Again, this is a gentle strik-ing, not a karate chop.

b) *Cupping* is done by forming a cup with the hand and then striking the body with the inverted cup. (Fig. 57) This produces a loud sound, and this stroke is the most deeply penetrating one of all.

c) *Slapping* is done with the fingers of the open hand. Strike with a gentle, but brisk rhythm. Some people use the entire flat-tened hand. Suit yourself but be gentle.

d) *Tapping* is done with the fingertips, one or more at a time. Using the very tip provides a harder and more deeply penetrating stimulation than you produce by using the pads of the fingers.

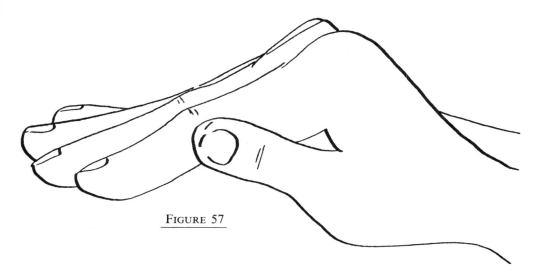

FIGURE 57

e) *Pinching* is done gently and consists of picking up tissue between the thumb and forefinger.

Be alert whenever you are using these methods, and use them
sparingly. Do not use these strokes on other people for your own
amusement, or to discharge your own tensions or frustrations.
Some people are so stoical that they will not tell you when you are
hurting them, so it becomes your responsibility never to exceed
your partner's comfort limits. If you are sensitive and caring, you
can tell whether or not you are causing pain. If you enjoy causing
pain, you are not yet ready to become a healer.

The mechanical model of massage calls for doing exactly the
same things on each side of the body. The difficulty with this is
that most people are tighter on one side of the body than they are
on the other, and therefore the tighter side needs more work. On
the other hand, some people feel "cheated" or out of balance if
they don't receive the same strokes on each side of the body, so I

usually do the same strokes on each side and then concentrate extra time and effort on whatever areas warrant them. By doing the regular strokes, I have theoretically relaxed and balanced both sides of the body; this should help the more involved muscles and tissues relax more thoroughly—and faster—when I begin to concentrate on them.

It is important to learn basic strokes because they help you understand how to move your hands and body in giving effective massage. But the strokes themselves usually only comprise half the massage; the other half occurs in time spent between strokes, connecting the major strokes together. With practice, you will be able to blend movements, to move from one stroke or area to another in a way that provides nourishing continuity to your partner. In massage, as in dancing or ice skating, once the basics become second-nature to you, you will spontaneously invent new ways of using your hands and body more effectively.

Always use your whole body in performing each stroke. Figure out a way to use your body weight, rather than your physical strength. And always define the body with your hands. This gets a maximum of work done with a minimum of effort. Remember to keep breathing deeply and freely yourself, especially when doing vigorous strokes.

BASIC BODY MASSAGE

What follows is a sample program designed to cover the body completely. There are, of course, many other strokes. This is intended to be an easy outline for beginners to understand, remember, and apply.

CAUTION: THERE ARE MANY CONTRAINDICATIONS FOR MASSAGE, WHICH HAVE ALREADY BEEN LISTED, IN PART, IN THE RULES SECTIONS OF THIS CHAPTER.

MASSAGE IS ONE AREA WHERE A LITTLE KNOWLEDGE CAN BE A DANGEROUS THING. WHEN IN DOUBT, USE POLARITY!

[Please observe the contraindications (#116, page 127). People with any of those conditions should not receive massage except under *strict medical supervision*. Therapeutic massage—which is much different from relaxation massage—should be done only by trained professionals who are fully aware of the person's past and present medical conditions.]

Massage should always be done with respect for the partner's body and personhood. Cover parts of the body not being worked on. Maintain a comfortable temperature in the room. The massage table should be covered with a sheet or towel, and your partner should also be draped with either a sheet or a towel. In some localities, there are laws requiring that the genitals remain covered at all times. Be sure to learn the laws in your own community. Ignorance of the law will not protect you.

Throughout the massage, visualize whatever you want to see happening. If you want the neck to relax, picture it! If you want muscles to unwind, see them (mentally) melting. What you do in your head is just as important—and maybe more so—than what you are doing with your hands. As much as possible, consolidate your intent on all levels.

Center yourself, as you stand at the head of the table. See yourself grounded to the center of the Earth by a golden cord which emerges from the end of your spine. See yourself surrounded with white light. Ask to be a channel for healing for your partner.

Ask your partner to visualize himself or herself grounded to the center of Earth by a golden cord coming from the base of his or her spine. Then ask your partner to visualize being surrounded by the healing energies of the Universe.

These may be pictured as green, pink, or white. Visualize this process yourself as you describe it for your partner.

You are now ready to begin. Enter your partner's energy field slowly. Use your intuition throughout the massage to comprehend your partner. But also *ask*, to make sure that your perceptions are correct. Be sure your partner understands that the purpose is to ease pain, not create it. Your partner should feel free to tell you immediately about any discomfort which s/he may be experiencing.

There are many acupuncture points on the head, and massaging the scalp and face will help your partner relax and enjoy the rest of the massage. Have your partner take three deep breaths before you begin.

1) Scalp

Gently lift your partner's head about two inches off the table, and, while supporting the head with one hand at the base of the skull, begin slowly massaging the scalp area on the back and the sides of the head. Some people are literally soreheads, so be gentle at first. It is astonishing how much pain can be stored here. Cover as much of the scalp as possible, and then switch hands in order to finish the part you had been using to support the head. The fingers of the hand doing the massaging should be bent slightly to form a sort of rake. The fingers can either move freely across the scalp or else can be planted rather firmly against the head and moved slightly in order to move the scalp itself against the skull. Be sensitive to your partner's reactions.

2) Face

You may, if you wish, oil your hands slightly before working on your partner's face. Do not apply oil directly to the face. Some people will not want you to use any oil near the face. When working without oil, go more slowly. And remember, in any event, that all facial areas and structures should be handled with care at all times.

Start at the forehead. Move from the middle of the forehead out to the sides, using the full length of each thumb. Do this three to five times. You can also make several lines across the forehead,

Figure 58

sliding the thumb lengthwise out from the middle of the forehead to the outer edges. (Fig. 58)

Lightly trace the eyebrows from the center outward, using your thumbtips or fingertips. Be careful; go slowly.

Using the heels of your palms, start at the middle of the forehead and go to the edge of the forehead and down over the temples. Circle around lightly on the temples several times. (Fig. 59)

Then go over toward the nose, under the eye, back out over the checkbone, down between the nose and lip, back out and down around the mouth, out to the middle of the chin, and back to the jaw. Repeat twice, trying to convey relaxation through your fingertips. (Fig. 60)

3) Neck

Use the fingertips to move as lightly as possible down the front of the neck toward the heart. Repeat twice.

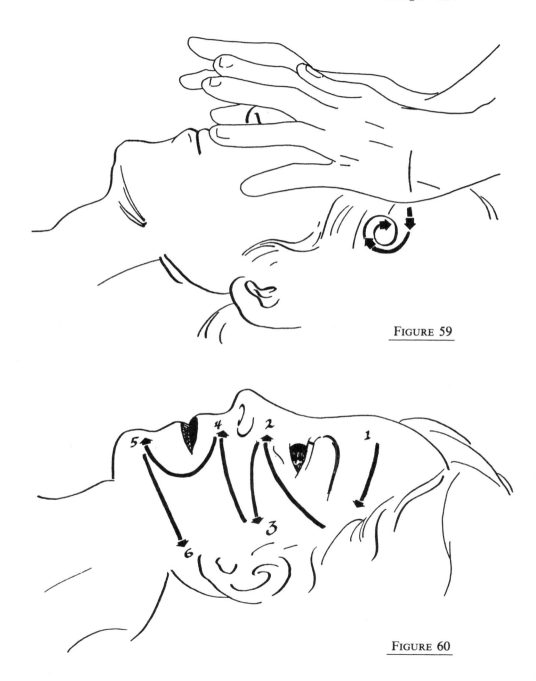

FIGURE 59

FIGURE 60

Now apply oil to your hands and rub it into the back of the neck and the top of the shoulders and arms.

The first stroke is done on the back of the neck and is repeated as often as you like. Partners often note an immediate increase in their level of relaxation. We all hold a great deal of tension in the neck and shoulders, so it is extremely important to help these areas to relax. (Simple finger vibration against the neck is also good, and may be used in preparation for the stroke.)

Place your hand under the neck at the bottom of the neck and pull upward toward the base of the skull, moving your whole hand. As the right hand reaches the base of the skull, the left hand slides under and begins moving up from the base of the neck. Continue alternating hands at least five times. Remember to put your whole body into the movement, and try to work as rhythmically as possible. (Fig. 61)

Lift and turn your partner's head slightly to the left and rest the skull in your left hand. Make sure the partner relaxes the neck muscles and lets you do the work of holding the head. Place your right hand along the right jaw and using light pressure, go down over the right side of the neck and out the top of the shoulder and down to the top of the arm. Using even lighter pressure on the return stroke, come back up to and over the shoulder and neck and back to the jaw. Repeat twice more. (Fig. 62)

Place your right hand at the base of the skull and gently roll your partner's head into your right hand. Then, using your left hand, do the same stroke on the left side of the neck and the left shoulder, three times.

Then lower your partner's head onto the table and repeat the first movement (alternating hands up the back of the neck).

4) Chest and Abdomen

Move to your right until you are on your partner's right, at the chest level. Apply oil to the entire chest and abdominal region.

Place your left hand lightly on the partner's right shoulder. Use your right hand fingers to cover the chest and ribcage on both

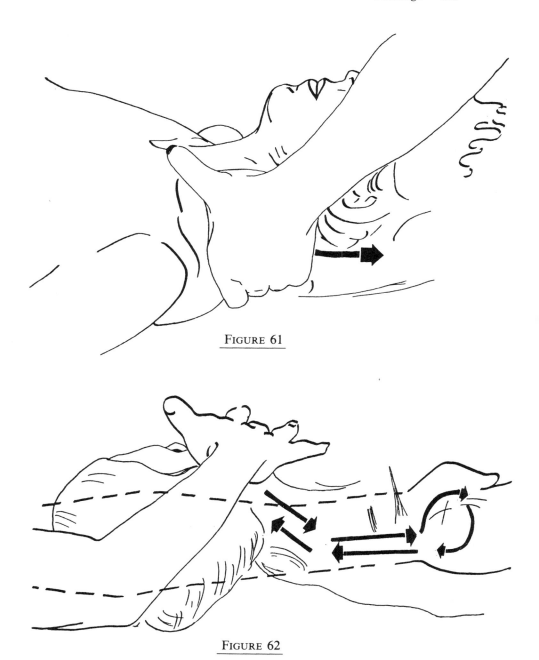

FIGURE 61

FIGURE 62

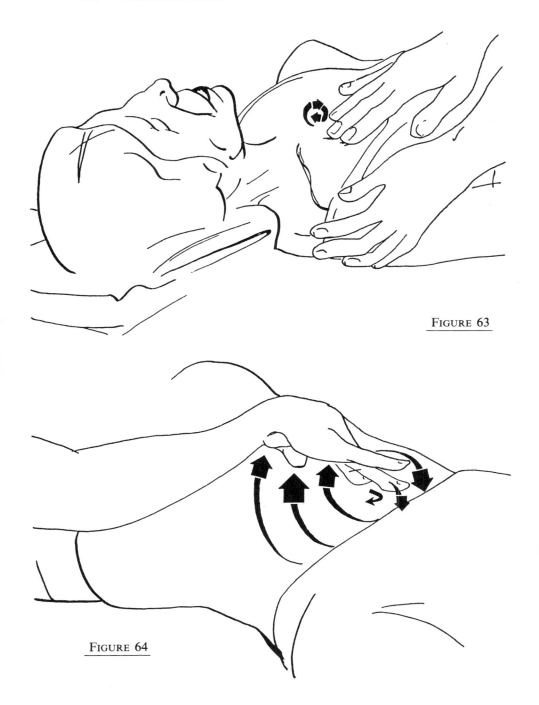

FIGURE 63

FIGURE 64

sides with a circular motion clockwise, making circles approximately two inches in diameter. (Fig. 63) Use light to medium pressure here, and be alert for soreness. Many people have little lumps or nodules, especially on the top part of the chest, which can become very painful when they are aggravated. Your partner can work these out, little by little, on his/her own. Do not press directly on the mammary tissue on either men or women. Many people are sensitive here, and some medications also make these areas tender in both men and women.

Always ask your partner to tell you what level of pressure is comfortable. People's tolerance to touch and pressure and pain is highly variable. Some people can easily tolerate heavy pressure. Others can barely stand the lightest touch. Some people have varying zones on their bodies: they may want light pressure on their arms, but very heavy pressure on their legs. Other people may seem very sensitive to touch one day, and very insensitive to pain another day.

Never presume to know what your partner wants; keep asking. In order to get the greatest therapeutic gain, you must match the level of massage with the level of touch which your partner's body requires at the moment. This may be light, medium, heavy, or variable, on any given day. In any event, always work more lightly on the head, neck, chest, arms, and abdomen than you do on other, more protected, areas of the body.

Once you have finished the chest, move down to the abdomen. Begin by placing your right fingertips just to the left of the navel. Make small clockwise circles with your fingertips to create a pattern of circles within a larger area. (Fig. 64) Gradually work around the navel, and then begin a second row, and then a third. The third will end down near the groin. Go back to where you began and repeat the entire sequence twice more. You may hear gurgling in the abdomen. This is good. It means that things are gently moving. Work carefully here. It is not necessary to go deep. Never work any deeper than one-half inch. Do not depress the skin any further than one-half inch.

FIGURE 65

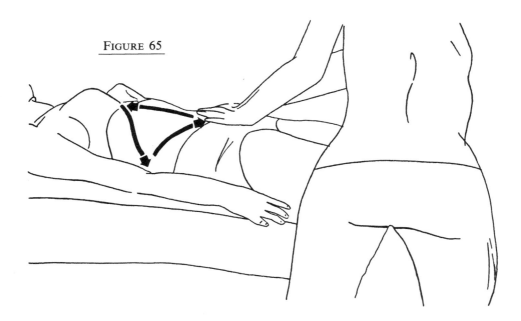

Then, standing down by the partner's hips, create a diamond on the front of the body. Go up the middle of the abdomen with both hands lying flat, side by side. Then one hand on each side of the body comes out along the edge of the ribs, down to the table, and back up toward the groin area. (Fig. 65) Repeat twice.

5) Arm and Hand

Using long strokes, apply oil to the right hand and arm all the way up to the shoulder.

You can use a Circular Thumbs motion over the entire hand, wrist, and forearm. With practice, your thumbs will become very adept at adjusting to different levels of tissue work and to the various contours of this part of the body. The thumbs work gently enough for this "thin" area, and yet they work deeply enough to effectively relax the underlying tissues.

To do Circular Thumbs, you anchor your hands on the body and then make circling motions with just the thumb. You may use one or both hands. To work on the palm of the hand, wrap the fingers of your right hand around your partner's hand so that only your thumb remains in the partner's palm. (Fig. 66) Now begin making circles with your thumb, applying pressure as your thumb moves away and using a lighter stroke as it makes the second half of the circle back to the starting point. As one thumb ends its forward stroke, the other one begins. (Fig. 67) Eventually, you will be able to establish a rhythm using both thumbs over the same area. Circular Thumbs are used in any small area or anywhere that tight muscles are found. Begin gently and then work more deeply as the tightness dissipates.

Once you have worked the entire hand, wrist, and forearm, place the lower arm and hand back on the table. Now, beginning at the wrist, place your hands sideways, facing opposite directions, with the palms downward, against your partner's wrist and forearm. (Fig. 68) Position yourself near your partner's waist area, so that you can easily move your hands up to your partner's shoulder (and back again) without moving your feet. Using medium pressure, slide your hands up the arm all the way to the shoulder. Use light pressure on the return stroke. Also use light pressure over the elbow. Repeat at least twice.

Next, lift the forearm and support it with your left arm while you work the upper arm with your right hand. You may wish to use Circular Thumbs here, too, because it enables you to probe easily and deeply into the muscle structures.

When you have finished with the upper arm, place the entire arm back on the table in a comfortable position, and move around the table and do all the arm procedures on the left arm.

6) Leg and Foot

Since you are already on the partner's left, simply move down from the arm to the leg. Using long strokes, apply oil to the left leg and foot. If your partner is very hairy, go slowly and use plenty of oil, rubbing gently and thoroughly to coat all of the hair. Failure to do this will cost you the goodwill of the partner.

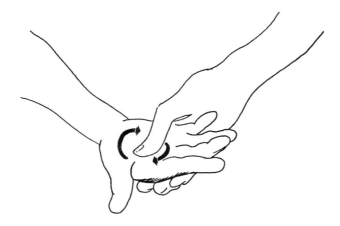

FIGURE 66

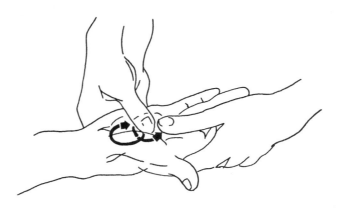

FIGURE 67

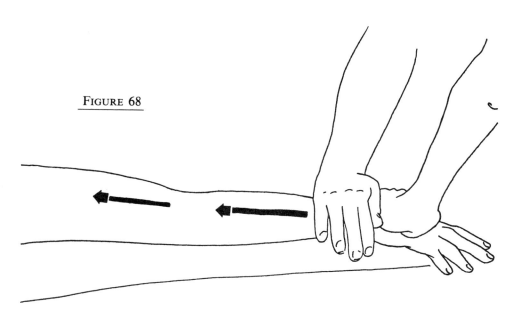

FIGURE 68

Begin with the foot. Bend the foot gently downward, toward you, to stretch the ankle. Some people are very tense here, so be alert. Next, push the foot upward, away from you. Then slowly try to touch the sides of the foot to the table. First try to touch the outside edge of the foot to the table. Most people can do this easily. Then move the foot in the opposite direction and try to touch the big toe to the table. People must be fairly limber in order to do this. Stretch the foot as far as you can, paying careful attention to your partner's face for any change of expression. If you are not sensitive to your partner's responses and reactions, your partner's body will refuse to relax. This is one reason why rapport between people is essential in massage. It is really the two of you working in concert which produces positive results.

Use your thumb to work the inside edge of the foot, which contains the spinal reflexes. Most people love to have their feet played with. Roll the foot from side to side between your hands, several times. Move each toe, first clockwise, then counterclockwise, three times. Be careful of the toes on anyone with joint diseases. Some people have very tender toes.

Use Circular Thumbs on the heel, on both the inside and outside of the foot. Then use Circular Fingertips over the ankle, top, and sides of the foot. Circular Thumbs may be very effectively applied to the bottom of the foot. Alternating thumb pressure may also be used. Cover the entire bottom of the foot, bit by bit, using the end of the thumb to apply pressure. Unless you have very strong thumbs, you will have to practice to build up this kind of endurance.

You may find a great deal of soreness in the ankle and foot region, so start gently, and glance often at your partner's face, watching for any change of expression. Soreness and pain here reflect energy blockages elsewhere in the body. (See chapters on *Reflexology* and *Polarity*.)

Once you have covered the foot, move up alongside your partner at ankle level. Position yourself so that you can reach from the ankle to the hips by shifting your body weight, but without moving your feet.

Now place your hands sideways, facing opposite directions, palms down, on your partner's ankle area. (Fig. 69) Using your weight to give yourself leverage, apply medium pressure going upward over the leg, all the way to the groin. Use lighter pressure over the knee, and use light pressure on the return stroke, as you pull yourself back, using your thighs and pelvis to center your weight. Repeat twice.

Next place your thumbs on opposite sides of the front of the knee, and move them back and forth in a semi-circular pattern around the knee. (Fig. 70) This feels wonderful and loosens up the knee and helps to relax the front of the leg.

Folding is very good to do all over the leg region. In Folding, you anchor the hand with the thumb, and bring the tissues forward with the fingers toward the thumb.

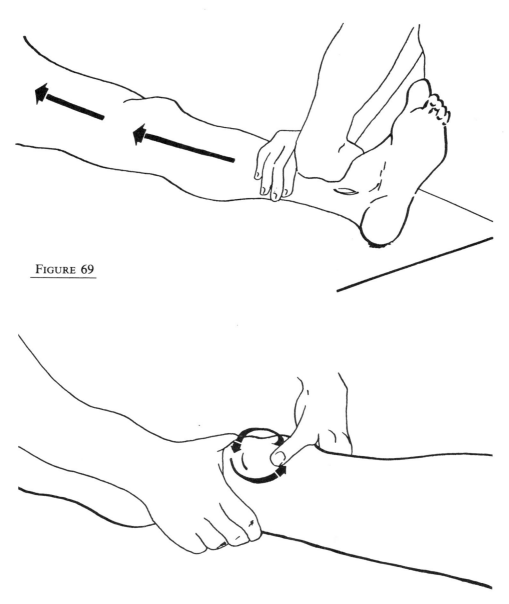

FIGURE 69

FIGURE 70

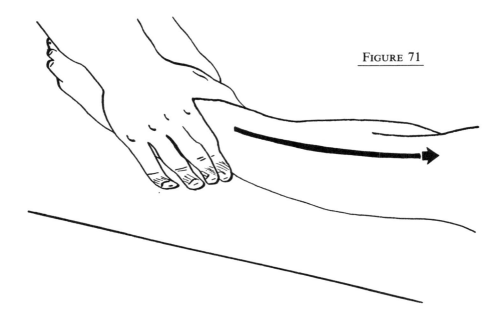

FIGURE 71

Fulling, using the base of the palm to stretch the muscles by moving them slightly in an outward motion, is also effective on the leg.

These two strokes can be interspersed with Circular Thumbs and Circular Fingers in order to increase the variety of techniques with which to cover the front and the sides of the leg.

When you have finished with the left leg, move around the table and do the same strokes on the right foot and leg.

7) Closing Strokes for Front

Everything so far has emphasized one particular part of the body. Now we want to put all the parts back together again. One nice way to tie them all together is with the use of the V-Stroke, which is done over one-half of the body at a time.

Begin where you are, on the right side, at the level of the feet.

Your elbows should be tucked in tight against your body, so that you can utilize your body weight.

Place your hands together in order to form a V. (Fig. 71) The left hand is placed higher because in your movements up the right side of the table, you will be leading with your left foot. The right thumb is covered by the left wrist.

Place your hands, in this position, at the top of your partner's toes on the top of the foot. Let your hands relax and mold to the body, and keep them as fluid as possible, so that they will move along easily, adjusting to your partner's body. Now begin to slowly move up over the entire right half of the body. When you reach the breast region, avoid the mammary tissue. You can divide your hands and go around the breast, or keep your hands together toward the center of the body.

Use your body weight, and shift your weight gradually, so that you take a minimum of steps, while maintaining an even pressure. Your pressure should be medium until you reach the heart area, and then lighter as you go up toward the neck and come across the shoulder and down the arm and hand.

As you reach the shoulder region and begin to go down the arm, your body pivots, because your right leg will now guide your body weight, and your right hand is placed in front of your left hand.

Now, once you have completed the first stroke (Fig. 72), which has brought you to your partner's fingertips, begin there and go back up to the shoulder area, using medium pressure. You are heading up the table, so your left leg and hand lead the way. At the shoulder area, shift your body weight and change your hands, so that the right hand becomes the leading hand as you go down the table, using light pressure on your partner's body. (Fig. 73)

Repeat the entire sequence, up and down, twice more. Then, moving around the bottom of the table to a similar position on the left side of the table, do the entire stroke over the left half of the

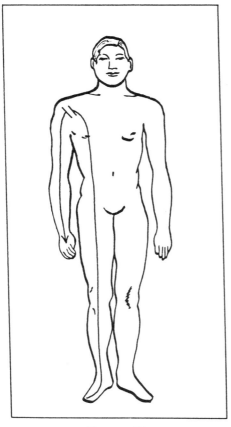

FIGURE 72

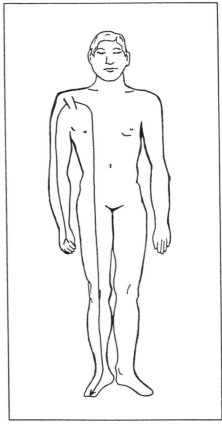

FIGURE 73

body three times. On this side of the table, the right hand leads the V going up the body, and the left hand leads coming down the body. Remember to shift your weight and hands at the shoulder.

To finish the work on the front of the body, use the Cleansing the Field Stroke from polarity.

Stand at the top of the table, and spread your fingers as you hold your hands approximately three inches above your partner's face. Imagine yourself pulling off static energy which your partner has released during the massage. Move your hands up off the head, and fling the energy away into an empty space. Repeat twice.

Now move to the right side of the table, near your partner's waist. Start at the waist and move up over the right side of the body, over the shoulder, and down the arm and hand. Shake your hands to fling the energy away. Repeat this motion of gathering and throwing away the energy twice more. Then begin at the waist and move down over the right leg and foot. Throw energy away and repeat twice.

Move to the left side of your partner and repeat the motions from the waist (upward and downward) over the left side of your partner's body.

This is a good time for both of you to take a break. Wash your hands immediately. You or your partner may want to use the restroom. Your partner may merely want to rest a few moments, and that's fine. It is highly advisable for you to sit down for a few minutes and to sip some water.

Taking a moment out will help you to re-focus yourself. It gives you time to reflect on the work just done, and to plan what you will do on the back of the body. Intuition may suggest an idea or stroke which would be beneficial for you to use with this particular partner.

Caution your partner to move slowly and carefully in getting up or turning over. Slow movements help everything stay relaxed. Fast movements can tense up the whole upper half of the body.

This is also a fine time for you and your partner to ground yourselves again and to see yourselves and the room filled with healing energies. Both of you can do some deep breathing to relax yourselves even further, in preparation for the work on the back of the body.

BACK OF THE BODY

After you feel sufficiently rested, begin the work on the back. Getting your partner comfortably situated on the table is the first order of business. Have your partner lie face down on the table. Your partner may want to have a rolled-up towel placed under the upper part of his or her chest. Some people cannot turn their heads sideways for any length of time. In anticipation of this, some massage tables have an adjustable headrest on the top side of the table.

Have your partner's body centered on the table, with the legs spread more toward the edges. This makes it easier for you to work on the feet and legs.

1) Leg and Foot

Begin on the side of the table by your partner's right leg. Apply oil to the back of the leg from the heel to the base of the buttock. It will not take as much oil on the back of the leg, because the sides were already oiled when you worked on the front of the leg. Then apply oil to the entire right buttock.

Return to the ankle area and position yourself so that you can reach from the heel to the base of the buttock without moving your feet. Place your hands, sideways, on the back of the ankle and foot, and use medium pressure on the upward stroke. (Fig. 74) Lighten the pressure as you go near and over the knee. Use light pressure on the return stroke. Repeat two times.

Then lift the foot and lower leg, and, while holding the leg, sit on the edge of the table so that you can support your partner's ankle comfortably against your left shoulder. (Fig. 75)

Use both hands throughout this next move, which is sometimes called the Viola Stroke. Begin by coming down the sole of the foot with your fingertips. You have to reach up to your left shoulder to do this. (Fig. 76)

Still keeping your fingertips parallel and close together, continue down over the middle of the calf. Just before you reach the knee,

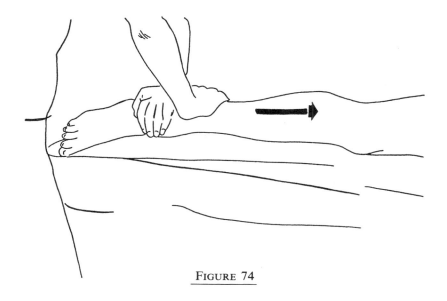

FIGURE 74

FIGURE 75

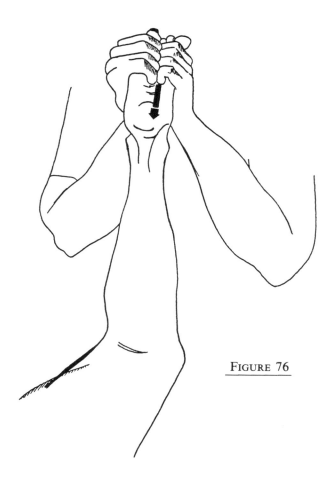

FIGURE 76

bring each hand out to the sides of the leg and come up the center of each side of the leg all the way back to the heel. Use lighter pressure on the return. (Fig. 77)

Then wrap both hands around the heel and ankle (Fig. 78) and gently squeeze down on all the structures as you use medium pressure moving upward on the leg. Your left thumb is about three inches in front of your right thumb, and the thumbs are on the

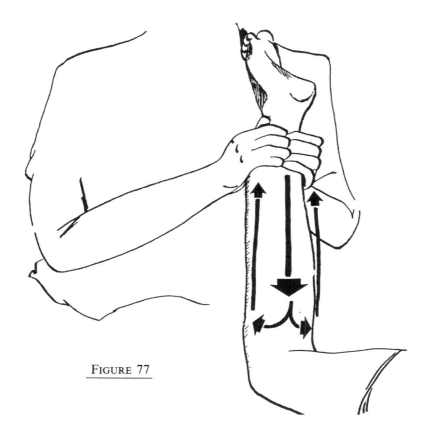

FIGURE 77

back of the calf, while the fingers are wrapped around the front of the leg.

As you reach the knee, place one hand on each side of the thigh, and continue upward. (Fig. 79) Move up onto the buttock, and as you do, place your hands side by side and circle the buttock three times. (Fig. 80) At the completion of the third circle, use lighter pressure as you bring the hands back down over the thigh, calf,

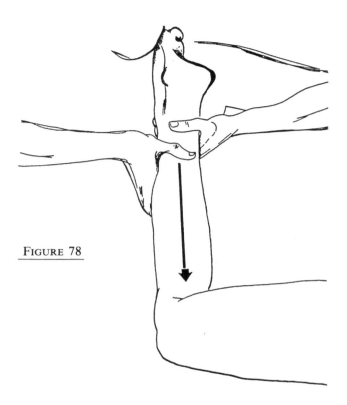

FIGURE 78

heel, and sole. (Fig. 81) At the heel, the hands turn so that the thumbs go underneath and the fingers come up over the middle of the sole. The ending position is the starting position. Repeat the entire movement twice more.

After completing the Viola Stroke for the third time, carefully get off the table and place your partner's leg comfortably back on the table.

Move around to your partner's left and do the same strokes on the partner's left leg.

2) Sacrum and Buttocks

Near the end of the spine, and between the buttocks, is a triangular-shaped fusion of several vertebrae known as the sacrum.

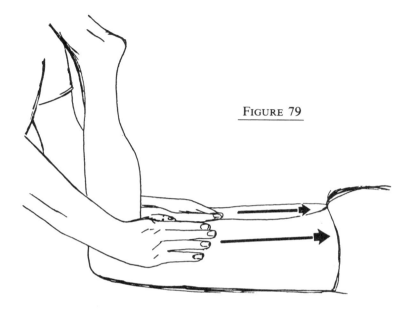

Figure 79

Place your left hand on top of the right hand and go around the outside of this triangle as illustrated (Fig. 82), using medium pressure. Do this three times.

You can also put pressure directly on the sacrum. Keeping the left hand on top of the right, apply pressure over the sacrum itself. Begin lightly and slowly increase the pressure to medium and then slowly reduce it again.

Next, work on the buttock opposite you. *Kneading* is good to open up the fibers of the buttock. Lift the muscles and knead them as if they were bread dough. Use both hands. *Folding* is also good: holding the thumb fairly steady, pull the tissues toward your thumb with your fingers. Using both your hands, you can also use a *Heel Press* to work more heavily here and to affect the deeper tissues. In the Heel Press, pressure is on the heels of the palms. Palms begin their stroke at a central point and move away from each other. (Fig. 83)

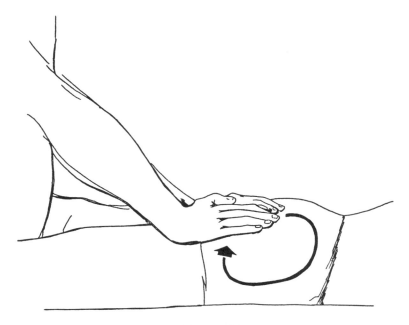

FIGURE 80

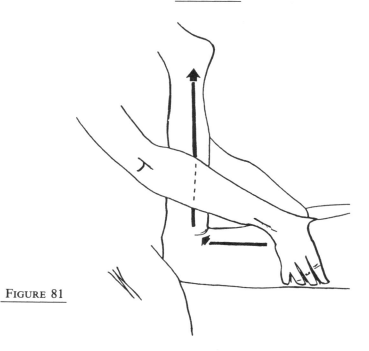

FIGURE 81

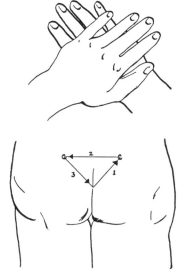

FIGURE 82

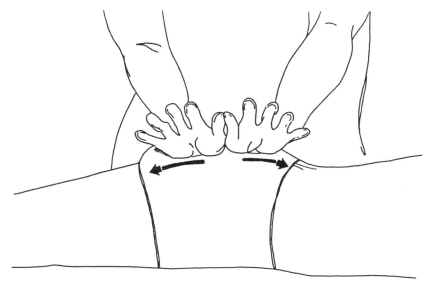

FIGURE 83

FIGURE 84

FIGURE 85

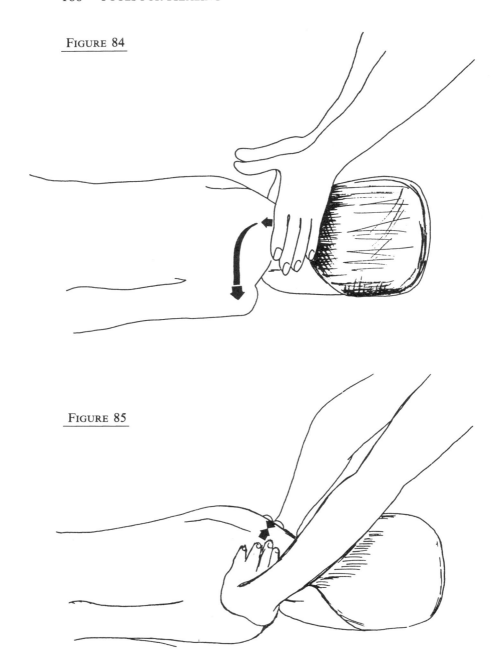

Use steady pressure and visualize the muscles stretching and re-laxing. Do this across the entire buttock area. Many people have a great deal of soreness in this location, so work carefully. For some reason, tension and toxins both tend to accumulate in the buttock region.

Circular Thumbs is another very good stroke to apply here to spread the fibers and reach the deeper layers.

3) The Back

First apply oil to the entire back, using long, gentle strokes.

One very relaxing way to begin or to end the work on the back utilizes a long stroke. Begin by standing at the top of the table. You are going to reach from your partner's neck to the bottom of your partner's buttocks. If you cannot reach that far from the top of the table, stand at the side, near your partner's head.

Start with the sides of your hands at the base of the neck. (Fig. 84) Your hands go out toward each shoulder, using all your body weight. Then turn your hands around and go in the opposite direc-tion, toward the center of the back. (Fig. 85) Move your hands un-til they become parallel to the spine and about one-half inch away from the spine. (Fig. 86) Center the pressure in your fingers, as you go down the back, until you reach the lower end of the rib-cage (approximately at the waist). After you reach this point, ap-ply pressure from the heels of the hands as you move down over the lower back and buttocks. (Fig. 87)

Circle the buttocks one to three times before beginning the return part of the stroke. Use your pelvis to pull your weight back on the return stroke. As you pull back, apply pressure through your fingertips. Come up over the sides of the back and up over the shoulder blades. (Fig. 88) Return to the base of the neck and repeat the entire sequence two more times.

Throughout this stroke, try to constantly feel the muscles under your hands. Be alert for any changes in the texture of the muscles. Sometimes one area on each side will be tight; sometimes one set of muscles on one side will be particularly tense.

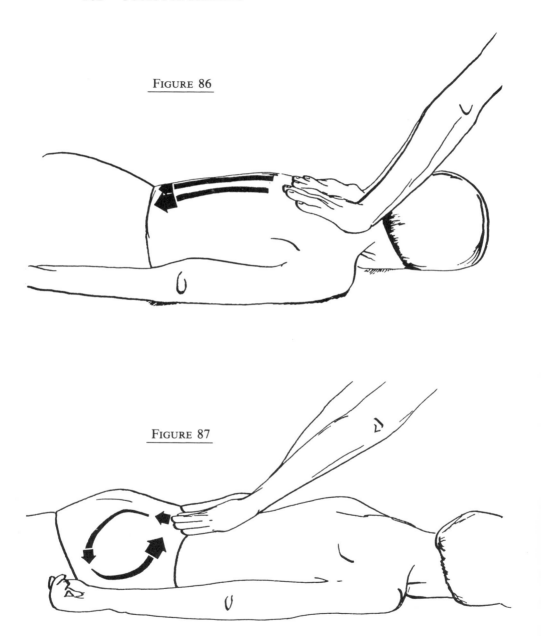

FIGURE 86

FIGURE 87

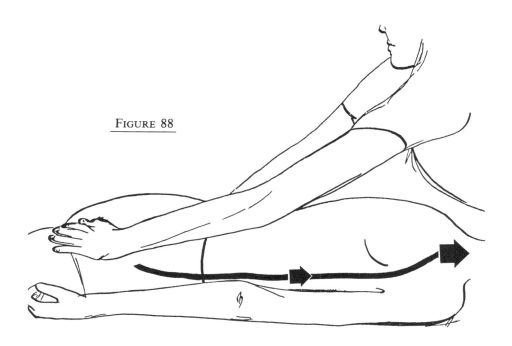

FIGURE 88

Many people hold tension in or near the spine; consequently, a great many massage strokes for the back emphasize the area around the spine.

Start at the top of the sacrum and work up along each side of the spine with *Circular Thumbs*. (Fig. 89) Then follow the same pathway with *Thumb Bands*. Start with your thumbs side by side, next to the spine, and pull in opposite directions. (Fig. 90) Overlap strokes somewhat, so that it takes about five series of strokes to cover the spinal column. Do this on each side of the spine, using light to medium pressure. Picture any tightness here melting away under your thumbtips.

Now start at the base of the spine, just above the sacrum, and do shorter Thumb Bands in the area one-half inch away from the spine. (Fig. 91) Here, the thumbs only move about two inches.

Work all the way up to the neck; then go around the table and do the same thing on the other side of the spine.

While there, you can do the *Planer*. (Fig. 92) Place the base of your left hand at a 45° angle alongside the spine. Start at the sacrum and come up along the spine. When you reach the shoulder, place your hand flat and use light pressure to come down the arm and return to the starting position. Repeat twice.

Next, turn your hand and place the base of your left palm in the groove on the side of the spine opposite you. This is the same groove we have been working with, which is located about one-half inch out from the spine. Use the Heel Press, which we used earlier on the buttocks. You want to apply pressure with the bottom of the palm while keeping the rest of your hand relaxed. Move the left palm all the way up the back and lift it off. (Fig. 93) Then set your right palm down at the spot where you lifted the left, and make the return motion with your right hand and arm. Continue alternating for several more strokes.

Afterward, still reaching to the opposite side, apply the *Scapula Triangle* to the shoulder blade (scapula) across from you. Stand at your partner's waist. Put your hands on the scapula and push away till your hands reach the table. (Fig. 94) Pull your weight back from your pelvis. The bottom hand comes up along the base of the shoulder blade and back to its original position while the top hand simultaneously comes back along the top of the scapula and then down along the spine until it reaches its starting position. Repeat entire stroke twice more.

Go around the table and do the Planer (45° angle), Heel Press, and Scapula Triangle on the right side of the body (while you are standing on the left).

If you noted tightness anywhere, go back to the involved area or areas. Light tapping or vibrating will help loosen the muscles. Do not apply heavy pressure over tight spots. Rub your hands together for ten seconds and place your palms over the affected area, letting the moist warmth of your hands penetrate. Maintain

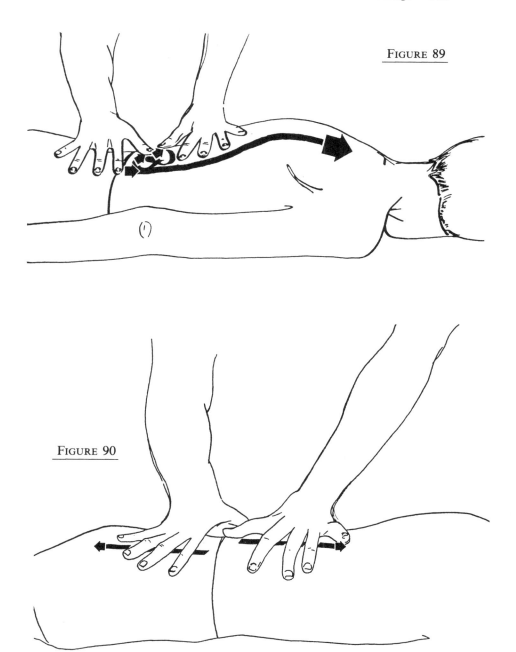

FIGURE 89

FIGURE 90

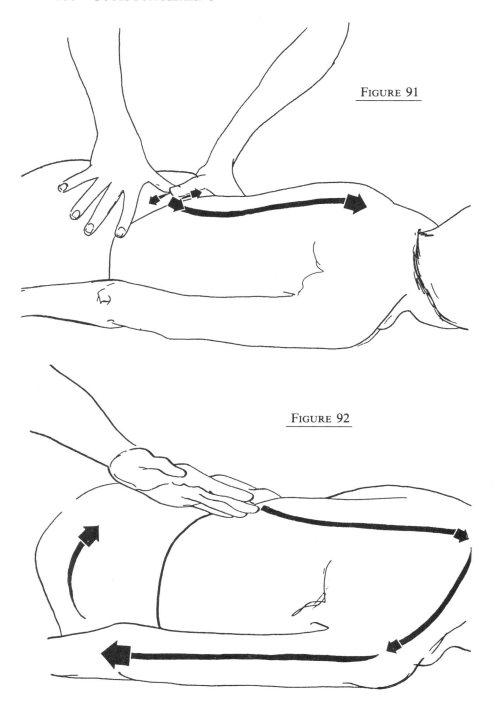

FIGURE 91

FIGURE 92

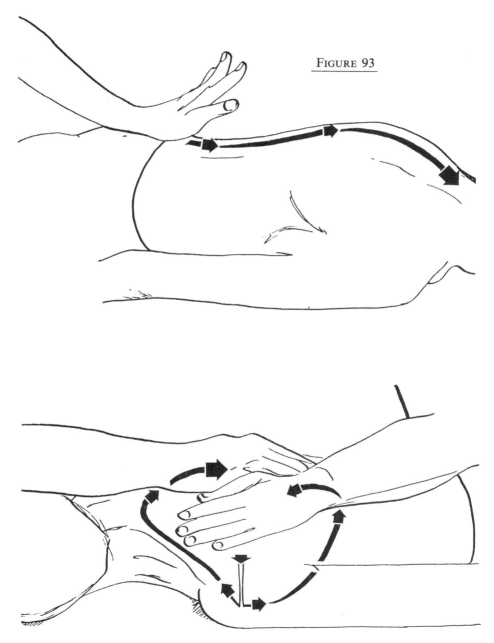

FIGURE 93

FIGURE 94

till the warmth in your hands lessens. Repeat twice. Let this area rest, and continue on. The warmth you have applied will eventually bring relief.

Now that the back is relaxed, you can do several things to help it stay that way.

The first is to apply *Hacking* to the back and buttocks, *except over the spine itself.* Both hands strike the back alternately. The object here is not to hit hard (which would hurt, and cause the muscles to tense), but to cause on-off pressure which first stimulates and then relaxes the muscles even more deeply than they were relaxed previously. Strike the back with the last three fingers of each hand, but do this gently—especially until you have practiced enough to be able to control both hands simultaneously. (You can practice on your own thighs.)

After you cover one buttock and one side of the back, move around the table and do the other side. Then make your hands into inverted cups and apply *Cupping* on that side of the back. Cupping is a very penetrating stroke which reaches deeper levels of tissue. When you finish one side, come around and do the other side. (You should now be back by the partner's left side.)

Apply *Tapping* to the entire back and buttock area with your fingertips, using both hands. Get a springiness into it, so that you almost bounce off the back even as you are striking it. Use a medium touch at first and gradually diminish so that you are really touching, rather than tapping, as you finish.

Position yourself near the buttock area in order to do the *Triple Heart.* This looks just the way it sounds. You make three hearts on the back. You will be reaching from the buttocks to the shoulders, so stand accordingly.

Begin with your hands parallel to the base of the sacrum. (Fig. 95) Move your hands upward, side by side, to the top of the buttocks. Then move outward, around the buttocks, and back to the starting point.

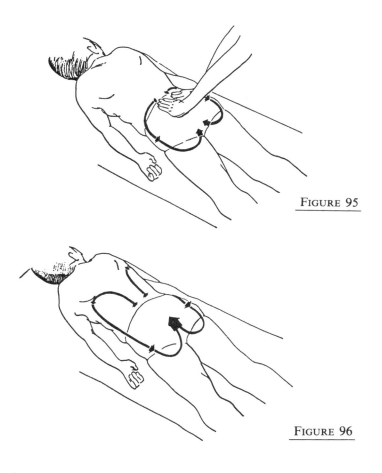

FIGURE 95

FIGURE 96

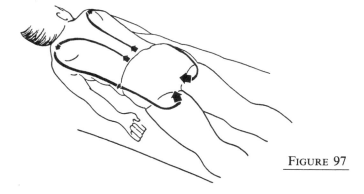

FIGURE 97

For the second heart, go up the back until you reach the area just below the scapulas (shoulder blades); go out each side, and back down to the original position. (Fig. 96)

To make the third heart, start as before, and go all the way to the top of the back, out across the shoulders, and down the sides to the beginning position.

Repeat the entire stroke two more times. The complete stroke is depicted in Fig. 97.

To close the massage, use the same V-Stroke and the Cleansing the Field Stroke that you used on the front of the body. Wash your hands immediately after you finish.

Your partner may want to rest for a few minutes, to let the full effects of the massage soak in. S/He may also want to use the bathroom before getting dressed. Both of you may wish to drink some water or herbal teas.

AFTERWORD

I hope that, in time, we will all be able to reach out in love and trust to help and heal one another through the wise use of touch. The preceding pages have tried to present the first steps in that direction.

I trust that what has been given here will assist you in healing both yourself and others. The secret in healing, as in every other art, is practice. Use these tools wisely, and well, and they will truly bring health to those who are ready for it.

May we all continue to share everything which these tools for healing teach us.

May balance and wholeness and growth be your constant companions.

REFERENCES

MUSCLE-TESTING

Diamond, John, M.D., *Your Body Doesn't Lie*. New York: Warner Books, 1979.

Lubecki, John, D.C., *Better Health Through Body Balancing*. Fair Oaks, CA: John Lubecki, 1982.

Thie, John F., D.C., with Mary Marks, *Touch for Health*. Marina Del Rey, CA: DeVorss & Company, Publishers, 1973.

POLARITY

Gordon, Richard, *Your Healing Hands: The Polarity Experience*. Santa Cruz, CA: Unity Press, 1978.

Stone, Randolph, D.O., D.C., D.N., *A Chiropractic Course in Structural Balance, Book IV*. Chicago: Randolph Stone, 1954.

_____. *A Course in Manipulative Therapy, Book II*. Chicago: Randolph Stone, 1953.

_____. *Energy: The Vital Polarity in The Healing Art, Book I*. Chicago: Randolph Stone, 1957.

_____. *Polarity Therapy, Book III*. Chicago: Randolph Stone, 1954.

_____. *Vitality Balance, Book V*. Chicago: Randolph Stone, 1957.

Acupressure

Cerney, J.V., D.P.M., *Acupressure: Acupuncture Without Needles*. New York: Cornerstone Library, 1978.

Chaitow, Leon, *The Acupuncture Treatment of Pain*. New York: Arco Publishing Company, Inc., 1977.

Chan, Pedro, *Finger Acupressure*. Los Angeles: Price/Stern/Sloan, Publishers, Inc., 1975.

Dalet, Roger, Dr., *How to Give Yourself Relief from Pain by the Simple Pressure of a Finger*. New York: Stein and Day, Publishers, 1980.

Mann, Felix, M.B., *Acupuncture*. New York: Vintage Books, 1973.

Tappan, Frances M., Ed.D., *Healing Massage Techniques: A Study of Eastern and Western Methods*. Reston, VA: Reston Publishing Company, Inc., 1978.

Reflexology

Ingham, Eunice D., *Stories the Feet Can Tell*. Rochester, NY: Eunice Ingham, 1938.

_____. *Stories the Feet Have Told*. Rochester, NY: Eunice Ingham, 1951.

Kunz, Kevin, and Barbara Kunz, *The Complete Guide to Foot Reflexology*. Englewood Cliffs, NJ: Prentice-Hall, Inc., 1982.

Segal, Maybelle, R.N., N.D., *Reflexology*. North Hollywood, CA: Wilshire Book Company, 1979.

Massage

Nichols, Frank, *Theory and Practice of Body Massage*. Bronx, NY: Milady Publishing Corporation, 1980.

Tappan, Frances M., Ed.D., *Healing Massage Techniques: A Study of Eastern and Western Methods*. Reston, VA: Reston Publishing Company, Inc., 1978.

SUGGESTED READING

Assagioli, Roberto, M.D., *The Act of Will*. New York: Penguin Books, 1974.

Bailey, Alice A., *Esoteric Healing*. New York: Lucis Publishing Company, 1972.

Berkeley Holistic Health Center, *The Holistic Health Handbook*. Berkeley, CA: And/Or Press, Inc., 1978.
_____. *The Holistic Health Lifebook*. Berkeley, CA: And/Or Press, Inc., 1981.

Besant, Annie, and C.W. Leadbeater, *Thought-Forms*. Wheaton, IL: The Theosophical Publishing House, 1971.

Davis, Roy Eugene, *An Easy Guide to Meditation*. Lakemont, GA: CSA Press, Publisher, 1978.

Edmunds, H. Tudor, and Associates, eds., *Some Unrecognized Factors in Medicine*. Wheaton, IL: The Theosophical Publishing House, 1976.

Jaffe, Dennis T., Ph.D., *Healing from Within*. New York: Alfred A. Knopf, 1980.

Karagulla, Shafica, M.D., *Breakthrough to Creativity*. Marina Del Rey, CA: DeVorss & Co., Inc., 1967.

Kirschmann, John D., *Nutrition Almanac*. New York: McGraw-Hill Book Company, 1979.

Krieger, Dolores, Ph.D., R.N., *The Therapeutic Touch: How to Use Your Hands to Help or to Heal.* Englewood Cliffs, NJ: Prentice-Hall, Inc., 1979.

Kunin, Richard A., M.D., *Mega-Nutrition.* New York: McGraw-Hill Book Company, 1980.

Leadbeater, C.W., *The Chakras.* Weaton, IL: The Theosophical Publishing House, 1972.
_____. *The Hidden Side of Things.* Adyar, India: The Theosophical Publishing House, 1977.

Lesser, Michael, M.D., *Nutrition and Vitamin Therapy.* New York: Grove Press, Inc., 1980.

Lingerman, Hal A., *The Healing Energies of Music.* Wheaton, IL: The Theosophical Publishing House, 1983.

Mann, John A., *Secrets of Life Extension.* Berkeley, CA: And/Or Press, Inc., 1980.

Meek, George W., ed., *Healers and the Healing Process.* Wheaton, IL: The Theosophical Publishing House, 1977.

Morehouse, Laurence E., Ph.D., and Leonard Gross, *Total Fitness in 30 Minutes A Week.* New York: Pocket Books, 1976.

Nichols, R. Eugene, *Picture Yourself A Winner.* Lakemont, GA: CSA Press, 1978.

Otto, Herbert A., Ph.D., and James W. Knight, M.D., eds., *Dimensions in Wholistic Healing: New Frontiers in the Treatment of the Whole Person.* Chicago: Nelson-Hall, 1979.

Oyle, Irving, Dr., *The New American Medicine Show.* Santa Cruz, CA: Unity Press, 1979.

Pearson, Durk, and Sandy Shaw, *Life Extension.* New York: Warner Books, Inc., 1982.

Powell, A. E., *The Etheric Double: The Health Aura of Man.* Wheaton, IL: The Theosophical Publishing House, 1979.

Rainwater, Janette, Ph.D., *You're In Charge: A Guide to Becoming Your Own Therapist*. Los Angeles: Guild of Tutors Press, 1979.

Schwarz, Jack, *Human Energy Systems*. New York: E. P. Dutton, 1980.

Shealy, C. Norman, M.D., *90 Days to Self-Health*. New York: Bantam Books, 1978.

Tansley, David V., *Subtle Body: Essence and Shadow*. London: Thames and Hudson, 1977.

Weinstein, Marion, *Positive Magic: Occult Self-Help*. Custer, WA: Phoenix Publishing Co., 1981.